NEW
TEXTILE
DESIGN

Judenpfad 61, 50996 Köln
info@feierabend-unique-books.de
www.feierabend-unique-books.de

Idea & Concept: Peter Feierabend, Marc Wnuck
Production: 12ender, Mannheim | www.12ender.de
Layout & Coverdesign: Sahba Yadegar | www.sahba-yadegar.blogspot.com
Back and Frontcover: Denise Boomkens | Spine: Fiorella Carla Cambareri
Printed in Asia

ISBN 978-3-939998-54-9

FEIERABEND
UNIQUE BOOKS

New Textile Design

In the wide field of design, the designing of textiles is regarded as a special discipline. It requires a deeper understanding of the technical side of the production of textiles as well as a specific knowledge of each fabric, of its uses, its properties and characteristics (dyes, fibres, and colourings). "New Textile Design" covers the many and various forms of the discipline. It includes clothing, caps, shoes, scarves, bags and appliqués, bedclothes, upholstery and lampshades. Even textile trinkets and other accessories are featured on the following pages.

The collected designs range from central motifs (on t-shirts, for instance) to patterns which often have to compete with the visible structures of the fabric. Additionally, the very form and manner of the presentation can become an interesting part of the work. Thus, we've included everything from sketches to elaborately staged photos. Motives, patterns, textures - "New Textile Design" covers the whole range of soft goods.

Textile Design

„New Textile Design" lädt ein zu einem Streifzug durch textile Welten. Die Gestaltung von Objekten aus oder mit Stoff folgt ihren eigenen Gesetzen und erfordert ein besonderes Maß an Kenntnissen der Eigenschaften und der technischen Verarbeitung aller verwendeten Materialien. Die Bandbreite des Textildesigns ist enorm: von Kleidung, Mützen, Schuhen, Schals, Taschen und Applikationen über Bettwäsche, Tücher, Polster und Lampenschirme ist alles denkbare vertreten, sogar Schmuck aus Stoff ist dabei. Neben Entwürfen mit Zentralmotiven wie etwa für T-Shirts finden sich unter den ausgewählten Arbeiten natürlich zahlreiche Strukturen und Muster, die nicht selten in Konkurrenz zur eigenen Struktur des Materials treten müssen.
Die Formen der Arbeiten sind nicht minder abwechslungsreich. Ob Skizzen, ausgefeilte Zeichnungen oder künstlerische Fotos, auch die Art der Präsentation wird hier zum Bestandteil der Arbeit.
„New Textile Design" präsentiert die ganze Vielfalt des Textildesigns – Motive, Muster, Strukturen. Alles, nur nicht langweilig.

content

clothing

jerseys, dresses
coats, suits, pants

Anne Rüter (GER) www.neoterisch.com

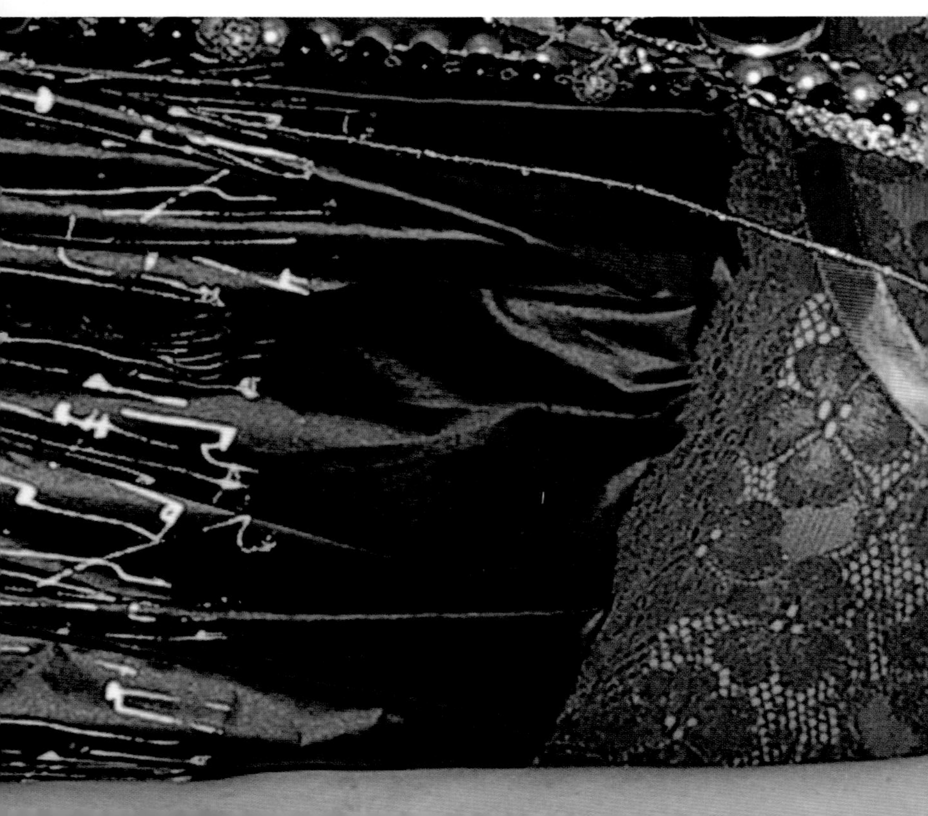

Jenny Kloszynski (NED) goplant@gmx.de

Tanja Meyle (GER) www.meylenstein.net

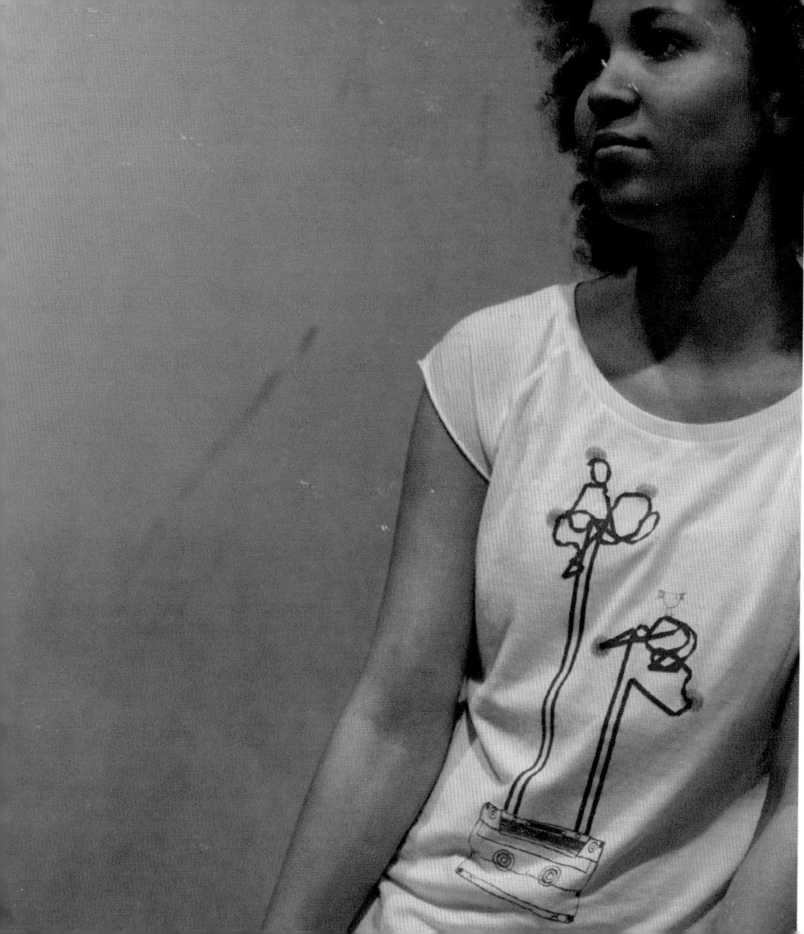

Silke Jaspers (GER) www.cfae-lala.de

Sabrina Vogel (AUT) www.sabrinavogel.com

Allie Boso (USA) www.noregrets.bigcartel.com

Florina Becichi (ROU) www.behance.net/florina

DEILANI

Florina Becichi (ROU) www.behance.net/florina

River Kuo (TPE) www.riverkuo.com

e prefer

half

River Kuo (TPE) www.riverkuo.com

half

is not only a store
but also b s the others
ideal pe ective and
lifestyle Thus we start
from t sp e as well as
sele ous half
attit ard life
through l discussion d subtle planning
PREFER to renew our
image et
all of y 09
with Easyg and Unique style
to aband e from daily life
why h
h - handwor armness and delicacy
a - art both o d distinctive aesthetic
l - lohas sp nic and pleasant life

 Josephine Kimberling (USA) www.josephinekimberling.com

Leslie Büttel (SUI) lesliebuettel@gmail.com

Josephine Kimberling (USA) www.josephinekimberling.com

Florina Becichi (ROU) www.behance.net/florina

DEILANI

Simon Stehle (GER) www.bloodgold.de

River Kuo (TPE) www.riverkuo.com

Aylin Tasoz (NED) atasoz@gmail.com

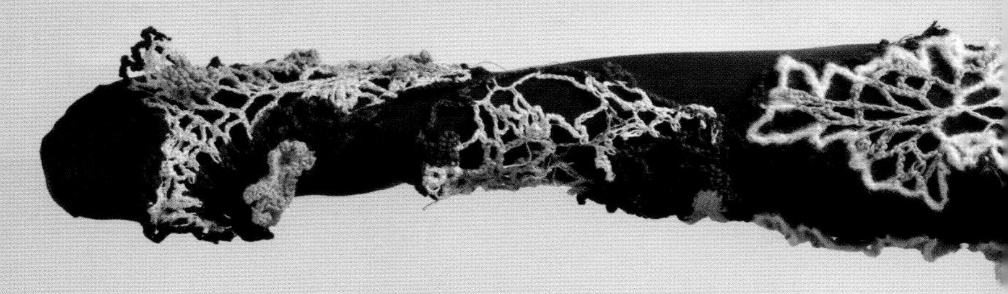

I
Hamilton

mercur
mercursenteret.no

Christian Frank Müller (GER) cfmrex@web.de

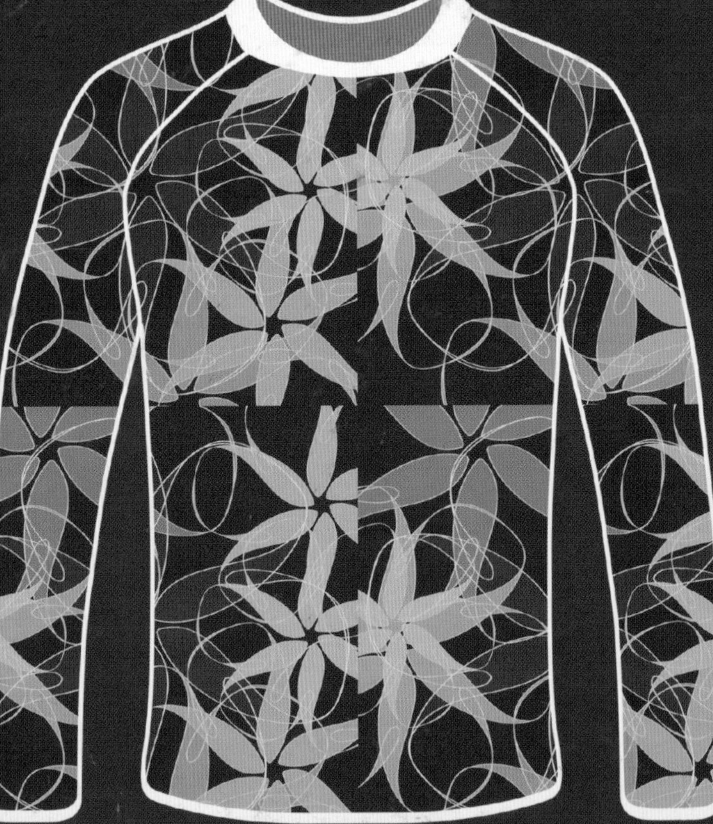

Vartan Tekneyan & Lilo Paleit (GER) www.ted-and-rose.com

sandra.marchionna@freenet.de

Circles · color: white-black · size: S-XL

Circles · color: black-pink · size: S-XL

Circles · color: violett-green · size: 36-46

Circles · color: green-pink · size: 36-46

Circles · color: black-pink · size: 36-46

CrossingWaves · color: violett-green · size: S/M, L/XL

CrossingWaves · color: green-orange · size: S-XL

OPTRIX
Spirals-color: black-pink-size: L*B 104*4cm
Spirals-color: green-white-size: S-XL
Spirals-color: green-orange-size: S-XL
Waves-color: blue-orange/violett-size: S/M, L/XL
Waves-color: green-orange/pink-size: S/M, L/XL
Waves-color: pink-white/green-size: 35-46
Waves-color: orange-pink/green-size: L*B 104*4cm
Waves-color: black-pink/white-size: L*B 104*4cm

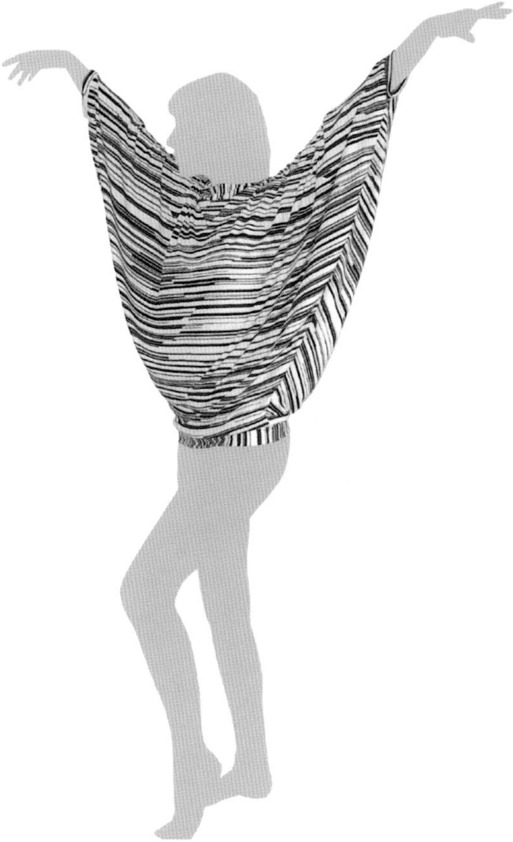

Tanja Meyle (GER) www.meylenstein.net

Lubov Malikova (UKR) www.flickr.com/photos/luba_ma

Silke Jaspers (GER) www.cfae-lala.de

Catherine Fayek (GER) catherine.fayek@web.de

fayek

Marc Prien (GER) www.empegra.de

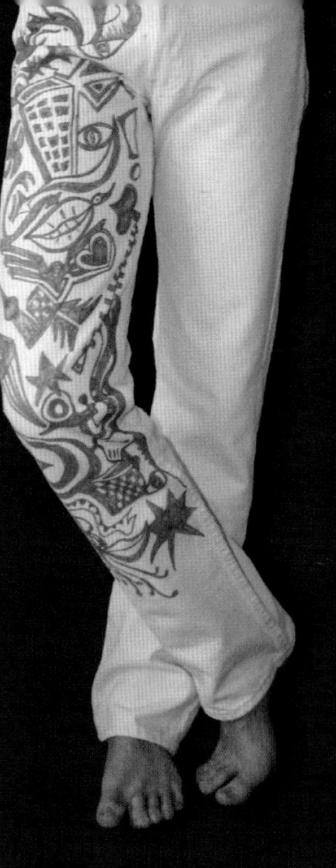

doodle
jeans

Aylin Tasoz (NED) atasoz@gmail.com

Mohamed Fouad (EG) www.fvad.deviantart.com

72 Ulla Gmeiner (GER) www.telaire.blogspot.com

Julia & Renata Franco (MEX) www.iqons.com/julia y renata

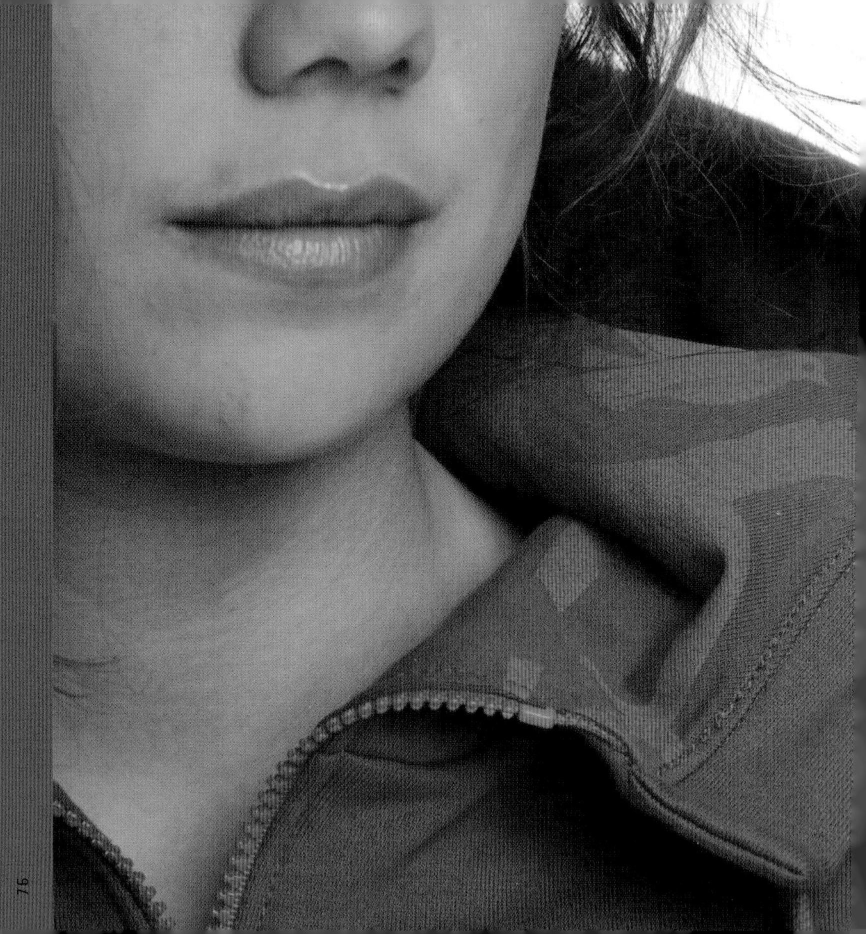

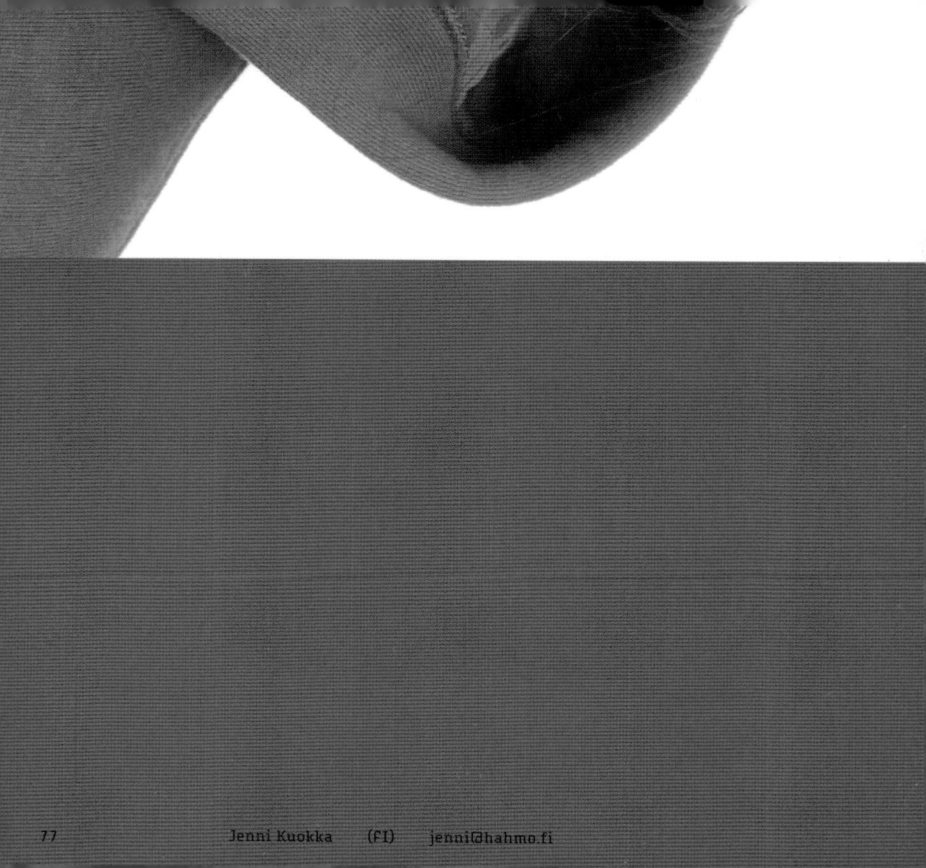

Jenni Kuokka (FI) jenni@hahmo.fi

Jenni Kuokka (FI) jenni@hahmo.fi

Vanessa Bauer (GER) www.sloverococo.wordpress.com

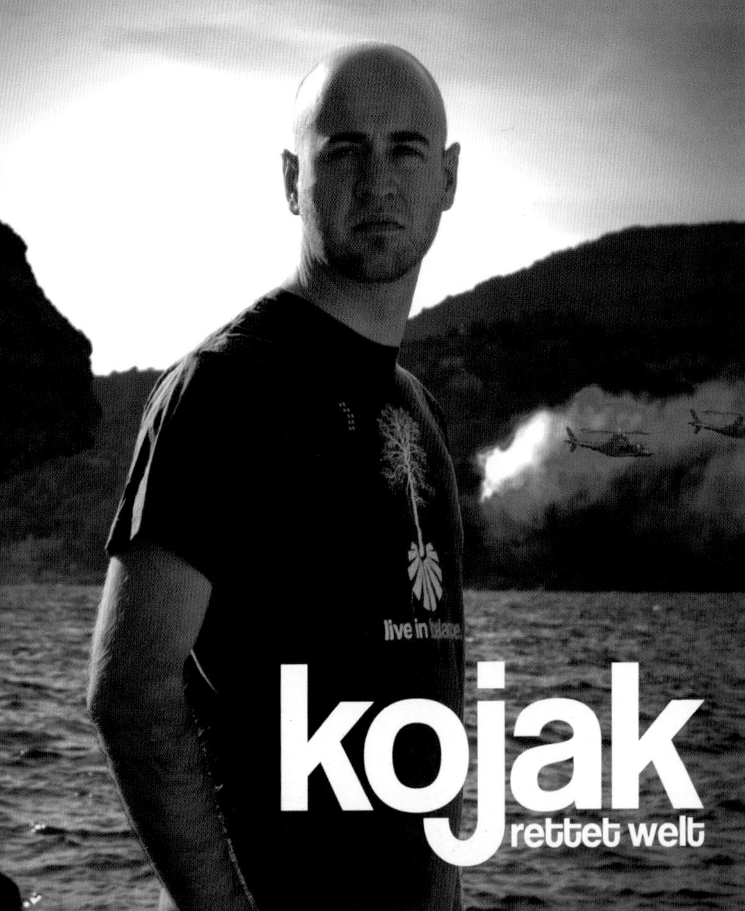
kojak
rettet welt

Nikolas Mauruschat (GER) www.omprod.eu

Magarita Pelaez (COL) www.tiendagula.com

Vanessa Bauer (GER) www.sloveroccoco.wordpress.com

Tanja Meyle (GER) www.meylenstein.net

Layko (Lay Sedlakova)   (SVK)   Lay.Sedlakova@gmail.com

B
A

Silvio Halleck (BRA) www.halleck.com.br

Vanessa Bauer (GER) www.sloveroccoco.wordpress.com

Kloszynski, Jenny (NED) goplant@gmx.de

Kloszynski, Jenny (NED) goplant@gmx.dew

kaneda (ITA) www.nosurprises.it

Fabrizio Paccagnella (ITA) www.spritzer.it

nynorsk
RESISTANT

Annette Eichler (GER) www.annette-eichler.de

nynorsk

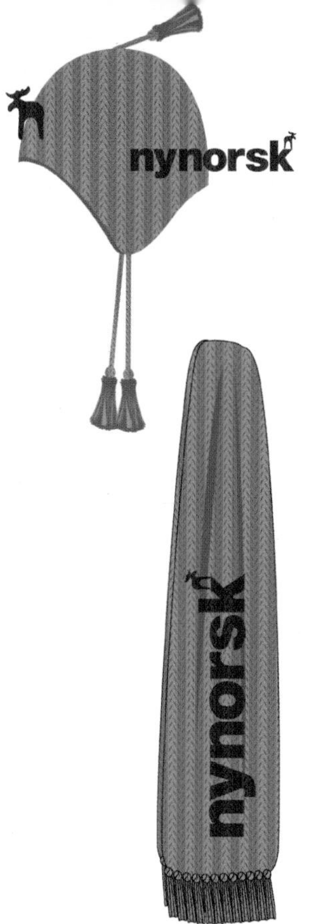
nynorsk
nynorsk

Alicia Villodres (ESP) www.alicia-villodres.blogspot.com

Suse Brand & Juliane Hoffmann (GER) susebrand@gmx.net

 Christian Frank Müller (GER) cfmrex@web.de

Sandra Marchionna (GER) sandra.marchionna@freenet.de

Spirals · color: violett-green · size: S-XL

Spirals · color: green-pink · size: 35-46

Spirals · color: blue-white · size: 36-46

Spirals · color: black-pink · size: 36-46

Zig-Zag · color: black-white · size: 36-46

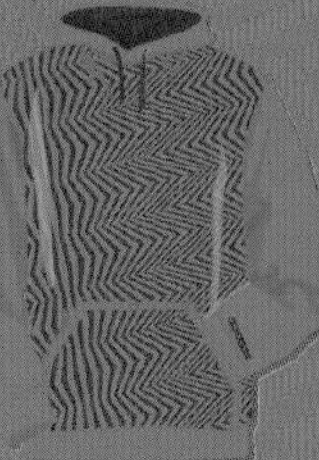
Zig-Zag · color: blue-pink · size: S-XL

Zig-Zag · color: green-orange · size: S-XL

DotLiners · color: violett-green · size: S-XL

DotLiners · color: white-black · size: S-XL

Metamorph · color: violett-green · size: L*B 104*4cm

Metamorph · color: green-orange · size: 36-46

Metamorph · color: blue-white · size: 36-46

Metamorph · color: grey-pink · size: 36-46

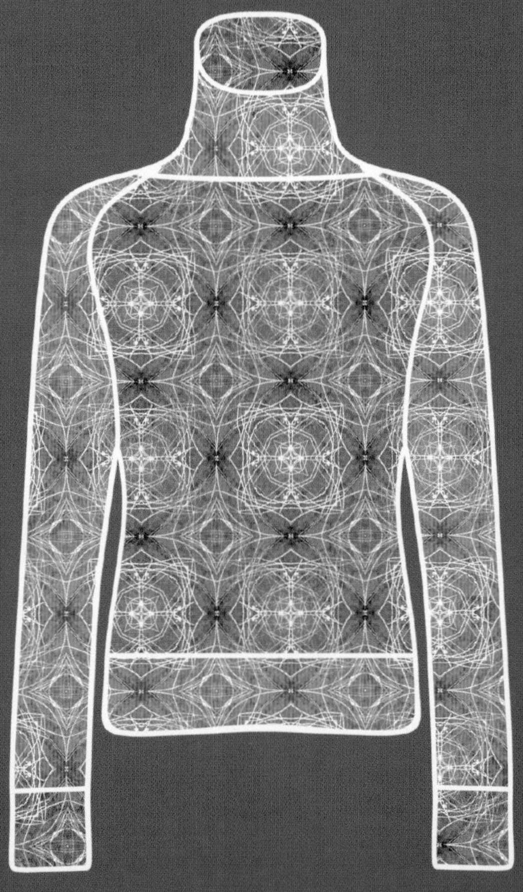

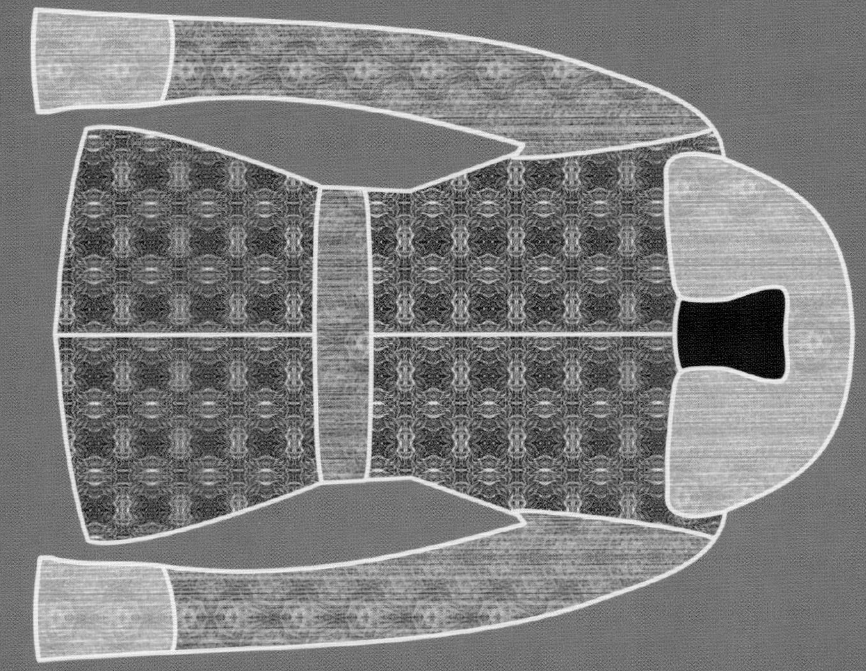

Vartan Tekneyan & Lilo Paleit (GER) www.ted-and-rose.com

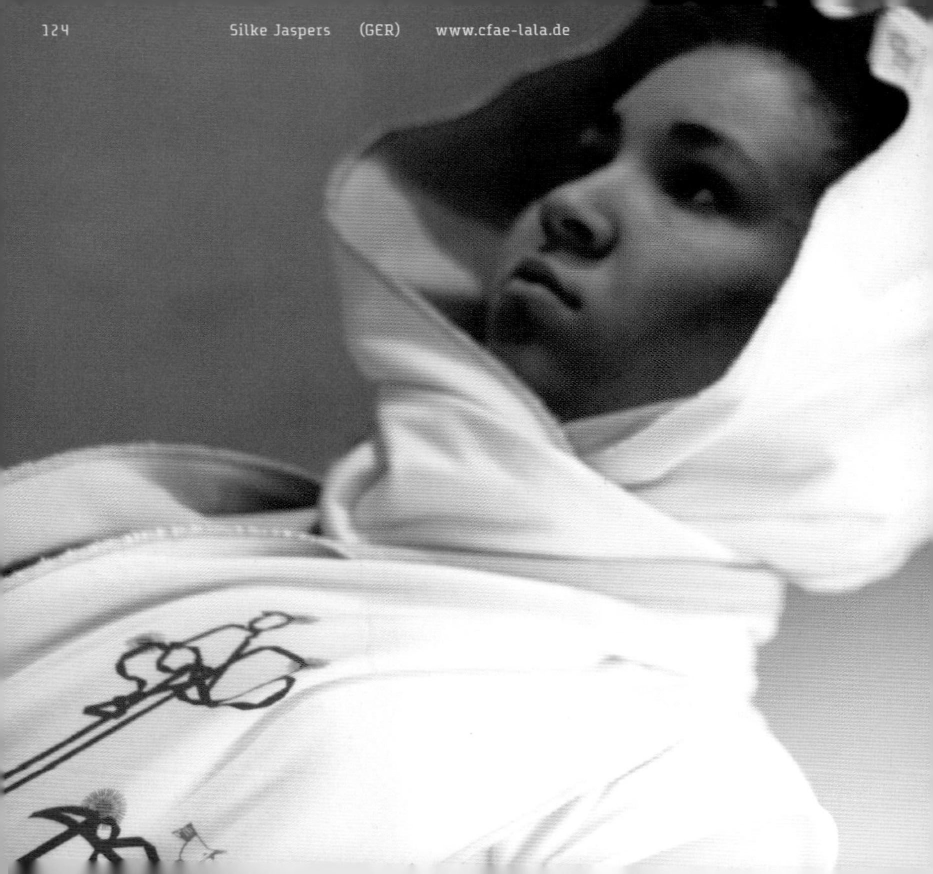

Mohamed Fouad (EG) www.tfvad.deviantart.com

Mohamed Fouad (EG) www.tfvad.deviantart.com

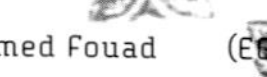

Mohamed Fouad (EG) www.tfvad.deviantart.com

Rebecca Fuchs (NED) www.casadelzorro.de

Yulia Yakushova (RUS) www.bangbangstudio.ru

Sabrina Goh (SIN) www.sabrinagoh.com

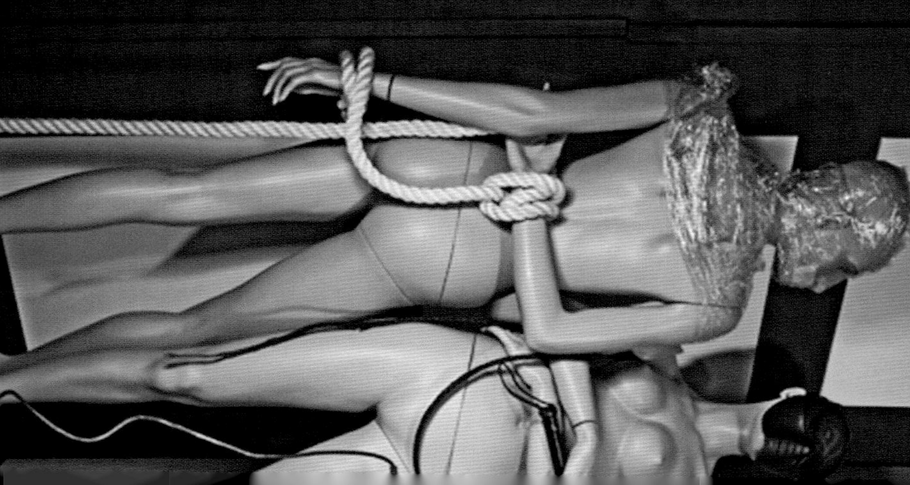

 Sabrina Goh (SIN) www.sabrinagoh.com

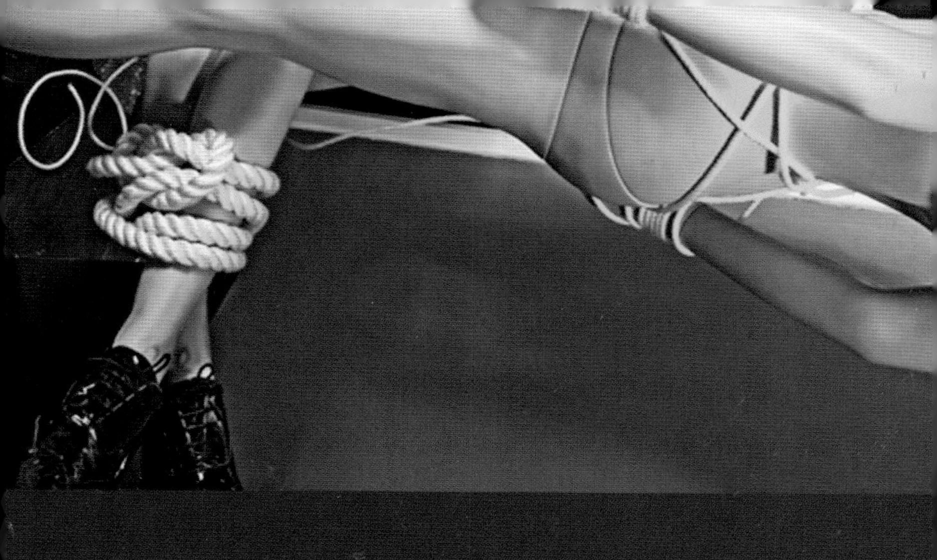

Sabrina Goh (SIN) www.sabrinagoh.com

Denise Boomkens (NED) info@deniseboomkens.nl

Eva Sichelstiel (GER) eva@sichi.de

© Jason Lear

t-shirt

tank tops, t-shirts,
girlie-shirt, sweat shirts

Pablo Fontagnier (GER) www.digitalplayground.de

FRESHAUSPRINZIP
THAT'S WHAT IT'S ALL ABOUT

 Pablo Fontagnier (GER) www.digitalplayground.de

FRESHAUSPRINZIP
THAT'S WHAT'S ALL ABOUT

Pablo Fontagnier (GER) www.digitalplayground.de

Pablo Fontagnier (GER) www.digitalplayground.de

Pablo Fontagnier (GER) www.digitalplayground.de

TOO MUCH
SHIT
THESE DAYS

sandra Hofacker (GER) www.apfel-z.de

OH my DEER
s'ware

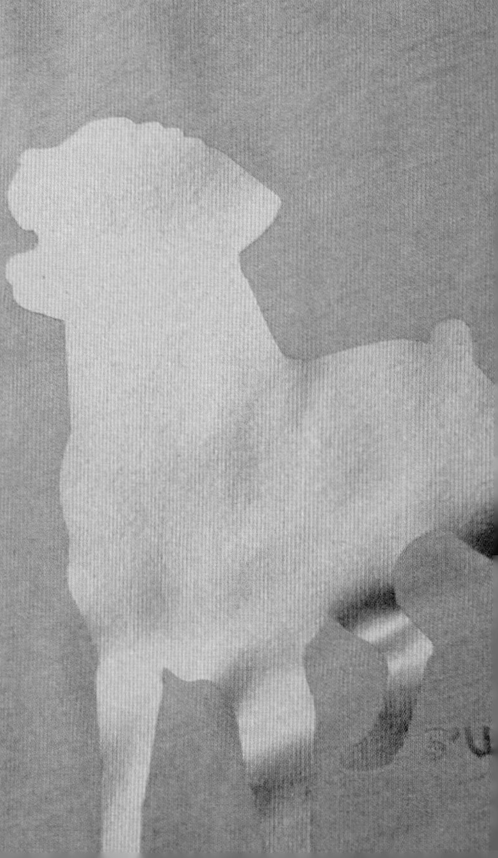

sandra Hofacker (GER) www.apfel-z.de

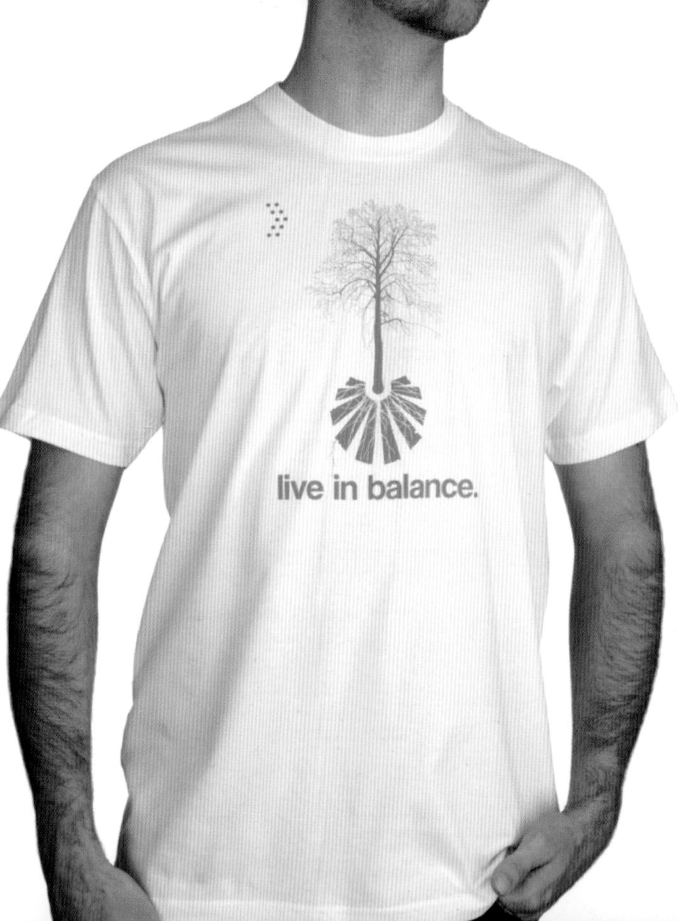
live in balance.

Nikolas Mauruschat (GER) www.omprod.eu

live in balance.

Dennis Schuster (GER) www.flickr.com/photos/dxtrs

hey!
Yo!
how are you doing

 Dennis Schuster (GER) www.flickr.com/photos/dxtrs

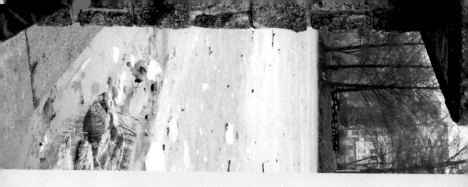

Philipp Zurmöhle (GER) www.phillennium.com

Jens Budny (GER) www.jensbudny.de

I
am
fish
ing

Matthias Tratz (GER) www.hkant.de

ÜBELST
PLUS
LES MEILLEURS

Martin Jordan (GBR) www.manss.com

0
100 Hz
200 Hz
2 K
Bass
1 K
500 Hz

Kama (INA) www.oxidizzy.com

OXIDIZZY

RiotCreations (GER) www.riotcreations.com

 Tomás Fliess (ARG) www.aupowerinside.com

Tomás Fliess (ARG) www.aupowerinside.com

Fluye

Tomás Fliess (ARG) www.aupowerinside.com

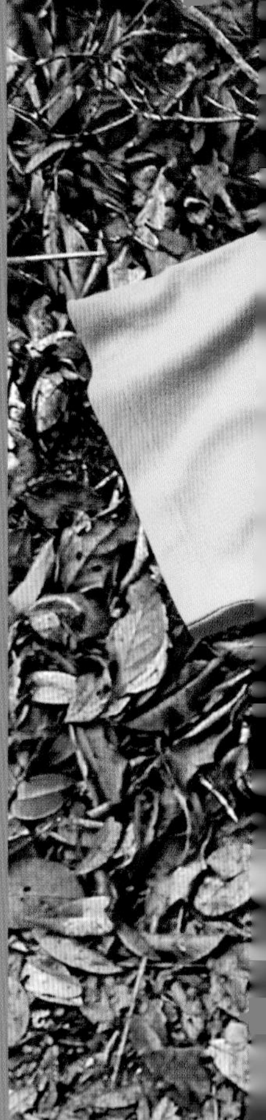

ss
au
sh
uo

Tomás Fliess [ARG] www.aupowerinside.com

au
au
ahora.

Julio Rölle (GER) www.44flavours.de

ZOO YORK
ZOO YORK
SLOW
ZOOYORK
SOFT ICE CREAM

Julio Rölle (GER) www.44flavours.de

OLDSCHOOLRÄP♥
COOL

Vault49 (USA) www.vault49.com

THIRSTY CROW TEE

ABANDONED
CLOTHING
CALIFORNIAUSA

Andre Weier (GER) www.nalindesign.com

Simon Stehle (GER) www.bloodgold.de

Nadja Girod (GER) www.nadjagirod.com

smil
AHOI

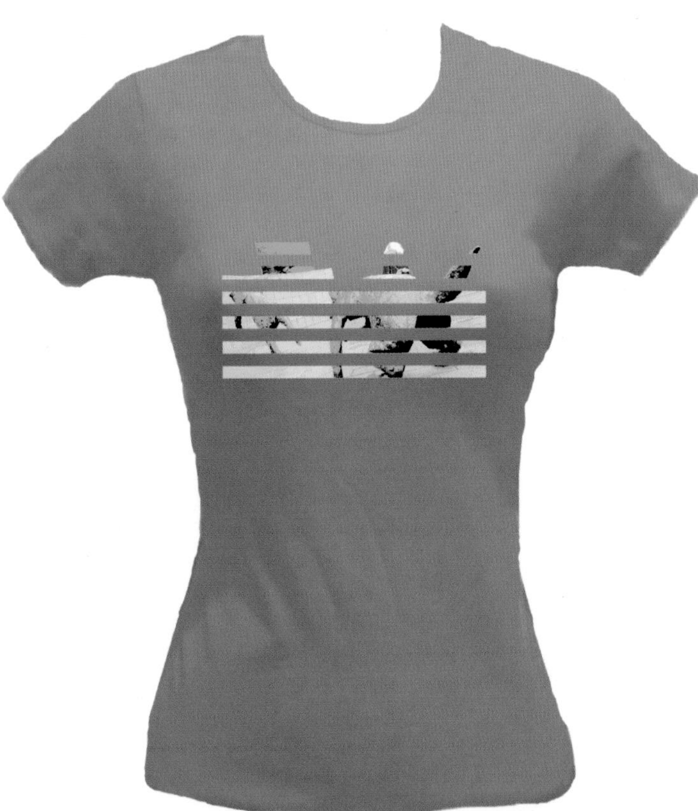

Rene Marquez (CAN) www.rene-marquez.com

linus von moos (SUI) www.ripsl.ch

Matthias Tratz (GER) www.hkant.de

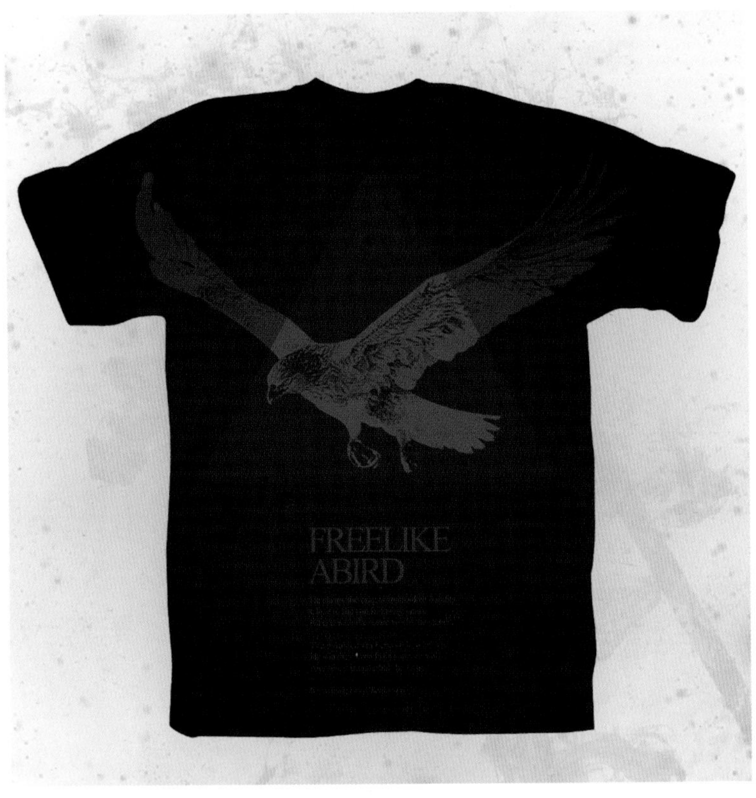
FREELIKE
ABIRD

Florian Kettner (GER) www.rv20.com

UNIQUE
STYLE

fluye

Harri Lemke (GER) www.designbuero-lemke.de

JAZZ
modern creative

Dennis Schuster (GER) www.flickr.com/photos/dxtrs

FRIENDS
&FREAKS

Kama (INA) www.oxidizzy.com

OXIDIZZY
HELLO

Mark Byk & Kristine Tortora (CAN) www.ampersandampersand.com

Galtsova Irina (RUS) irina.galtsova@gmail.com

Finna Leibenguthi (GER) www.wg-atelier.de

Love
paper
birds

Julio Rölle (GER) www.44flavours.de

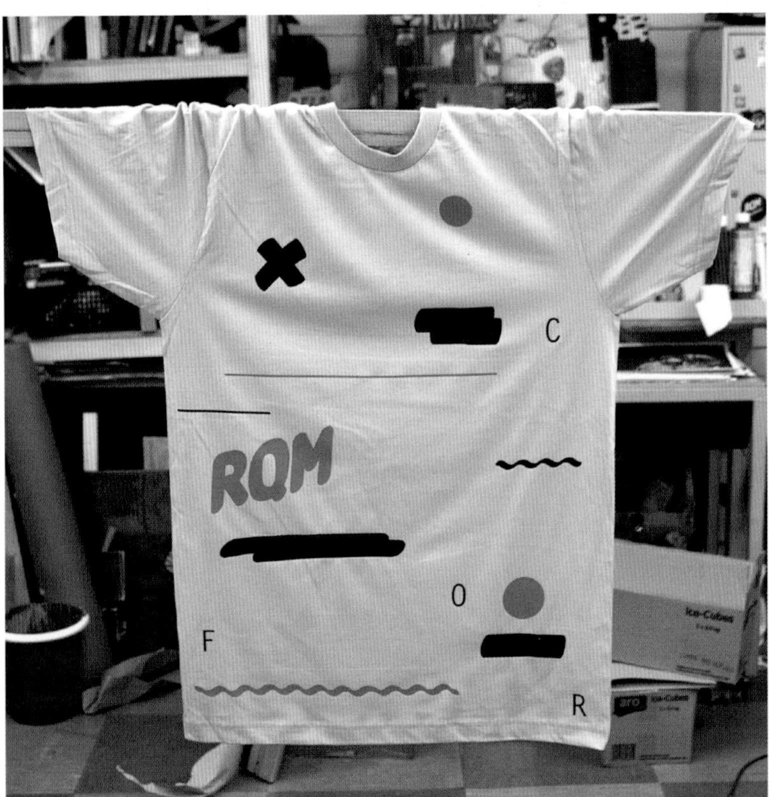

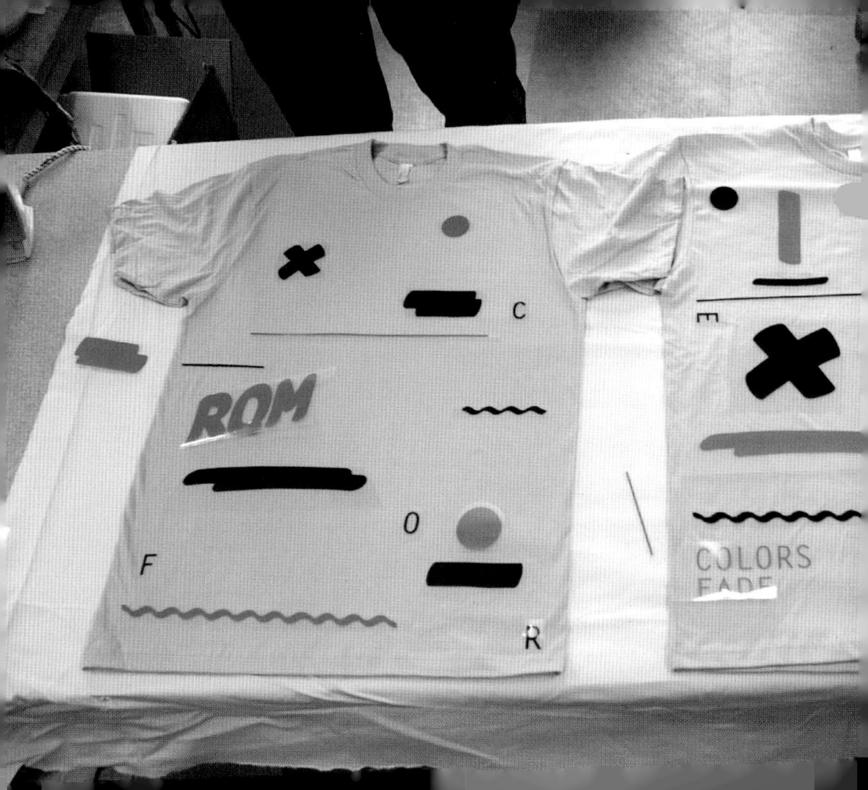
C
ROM
O
F
R
COLORS

Dennis Schuster (GER) www.flickr.com/photos/dxtrs

let the good times roll

Dennis Schuster (GER) www.flickr.com/photos/dxtrs

Sabrina Müller (GER) www.sabrinamueller.com

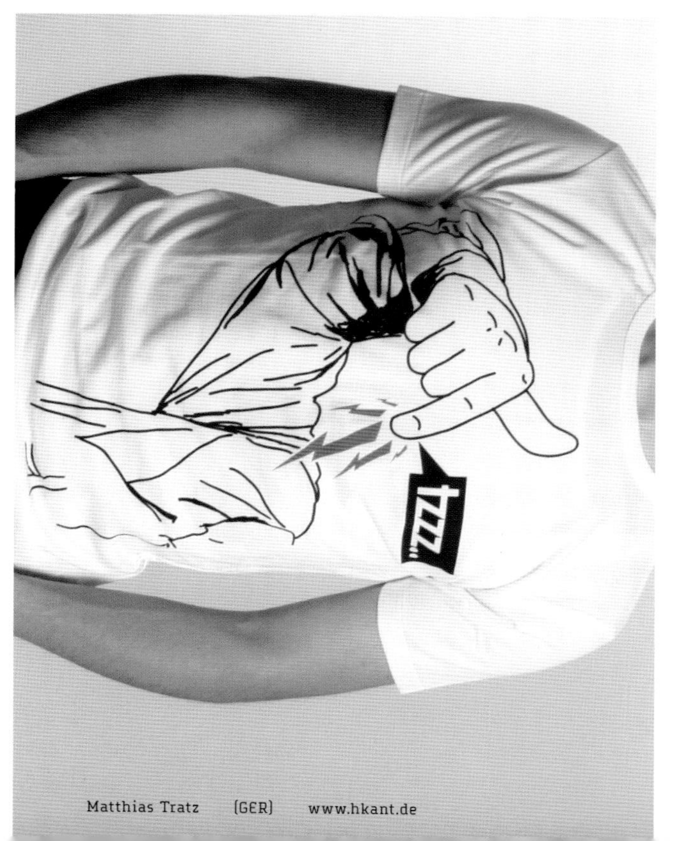

Matthias Tratz (GER) www.hkant.de

Philipp Zurmöhle (GER) www.phillennium.com

Kai Schroeder (GER) ks-schroeder@gmx.de

nobatik
anti berlin

Reclaim your City
anti
berlin
nobatik

Nerk collective (ITA) www.nerk.it

Nikolas Mauruschat (GER) www.omprod.eu

Mike Friedrich (GER) www.mike-friedrich.com

Dennis Schuster (GER) www.flickr.com/photos/dxtrs

Dennis Schuster (GER) www.flickr.com/photos/dxtrs

POLICE
OFFICER ONE
YOU'RE UNDER ARREST
CAUSE YOU'RE THE BEST

Simon Stehle (GER) www.bloodgold.de

M
OXIDIZZY

Kama (INA) www.oxidizzy.com

THIRSTY CROW TEE

Andre Weier (GER) www.nalindesign.com

44FLAV
OURS

44FLAV
OURS

Perfect Blend
Group

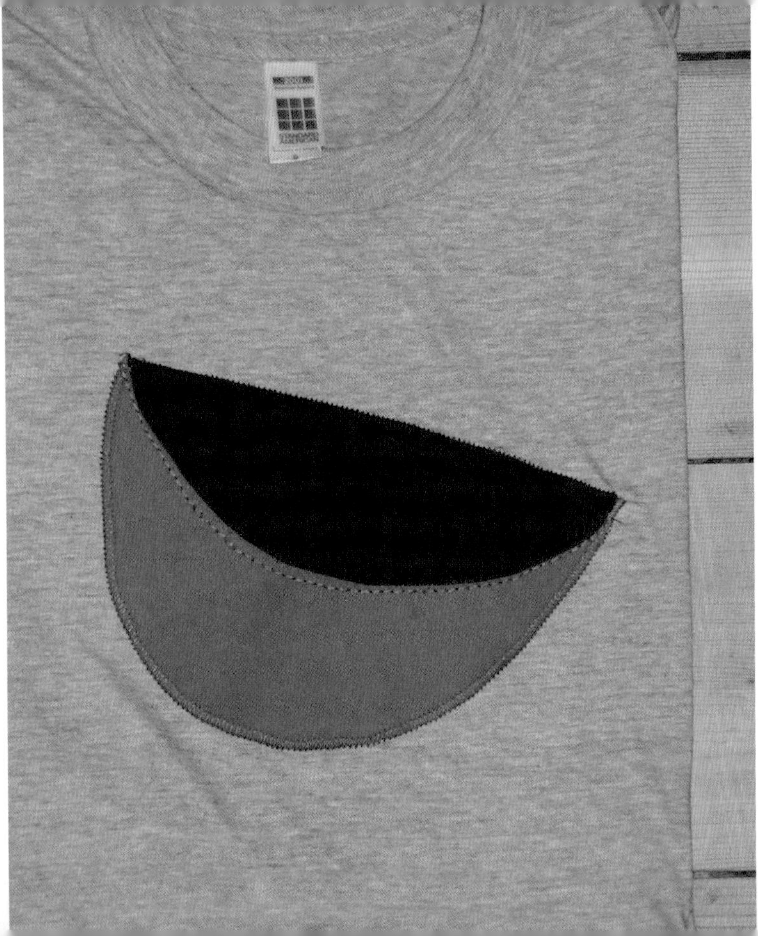

Julio Rölle (GER) www.44flavours.de

Sandra Hofacker (SUI) www.apfel-z.de

RADIO
VJING!
Graffiti

Julio Rölle (GER) www.44flavours.de

Julio Rölle (GER) www.44flavours.de

Florian Kettner (GER) www.rv20.com

A
armonía

Tomás Fliess (ARG) www.aupowerinside.com

Tomás Fliess (ARG) www.aupowerinside.com

Isa Hartikainen (GER) isa.hartikainen@gmail.com

glows
in the
dark!

Support
Your Local
Sneaker
Dealer!

Alex Knaack (GER) www.bxp.bigcartel.com

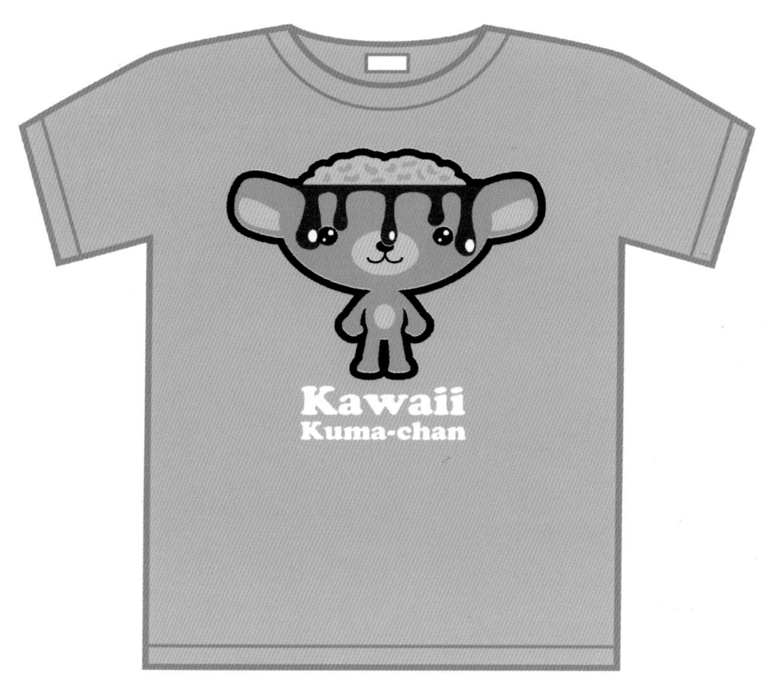

Ivan Ricci (ITA) www.kawaii-style.net

Matthias Tratz (GER) www.hkant.de

Nikolas Mauruschat (GER) www.omprod.eu

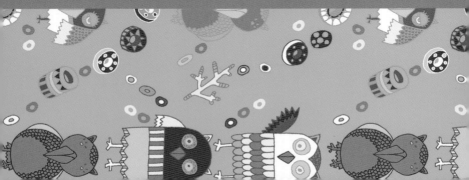

Marie Jacobi (GER) www.marie-jacobi.de

nobatik
antiberlin

aer (TW) www.flickr.com/photos/cotton120

aer (TW) www.flickr.com/photos/cotton120

Attila Szamosi (GER) www.peachbeach.de

Yummy!

MOTORCYCLE
HELLRAISER
CLUB
VELODROM
An epic
Fight

omprod

Nikolas Mauruschat (GER) www.omprod.eu

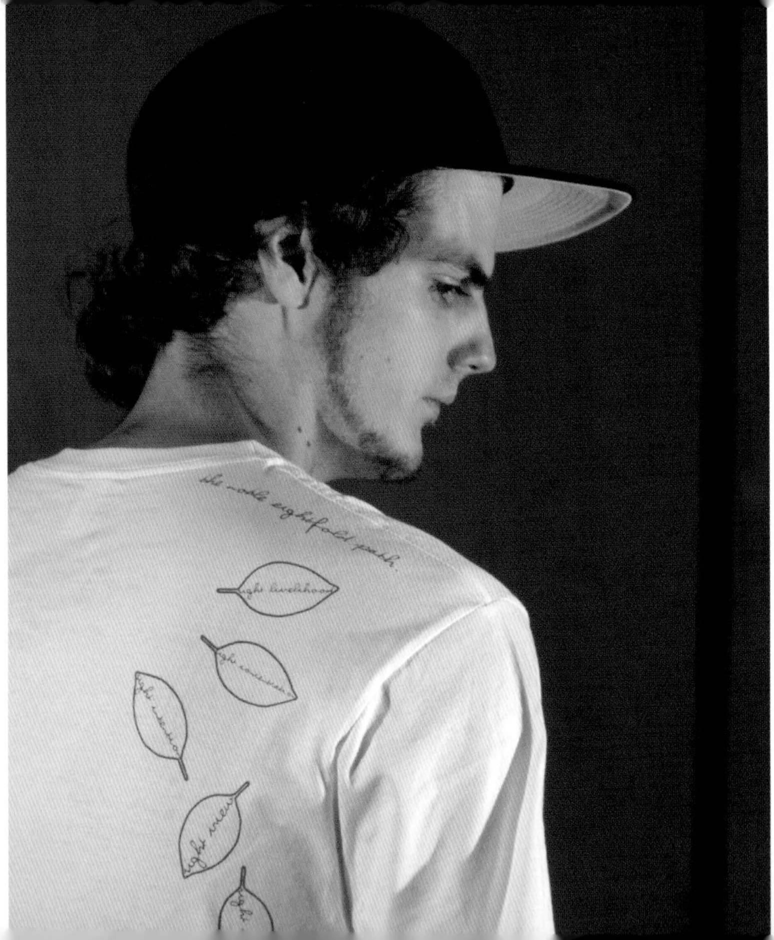

omprod
the noble eightfold path.

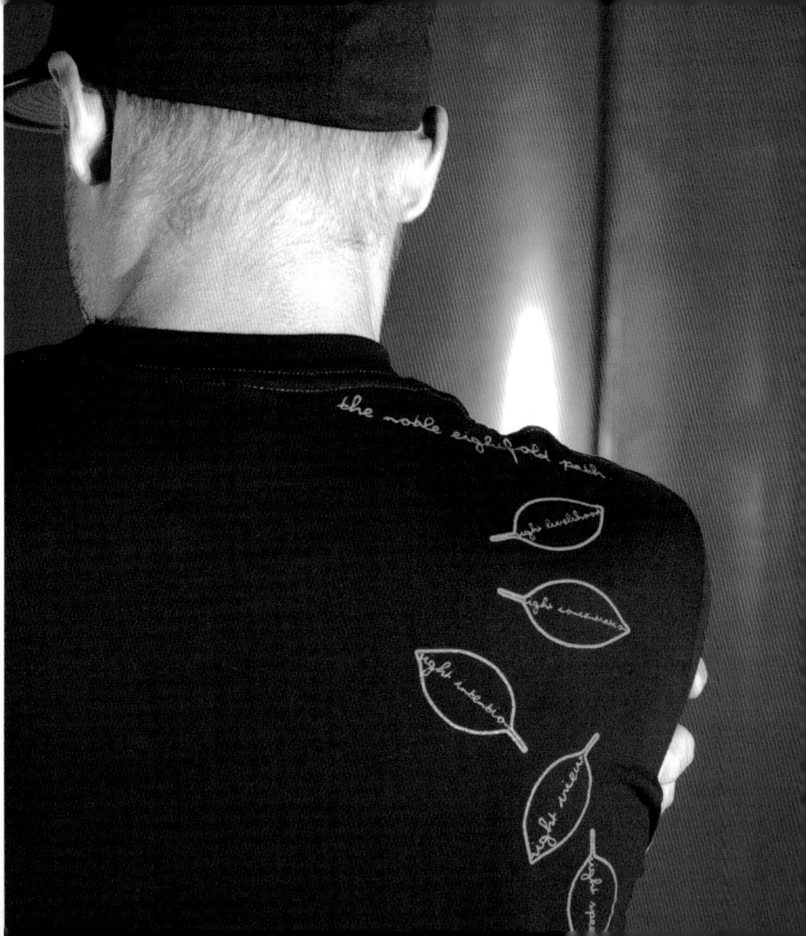

Nikolas Mauruschat (GER) www.omprod.eu

omprod
the noble eightfold path.

Nikolas Mauruschat (GER) www.omprod.eu

Attila Szamosi (GER) www.peachbeach.de

Every
thing
is ok
GLOBAL WARMING

Attila Szamosi (GER) www.peachbeach.de

JIMMY the LYNX
LOVE
IS
SPREADING
to the
WHOLE WORLD!

Attila Szamosi (GER) www.peachbeach.de

Attila Szamosi (GER) www.peachbeach.de

Attila Szamosi (GER) www.peachbeach.de

Attila Szamosi (GER) www.peachbeach.de

Wake up!

Attila Szamosi (GER) www.peachbeach.de

Attila Szamosi (GER) www.peachbeach.de

RiotCreations (GER) www.riotcreations.com

SOIL SOUND

holy

When life gives you lemons

WHALERIDER

THE
INVASION

RiotActivist
Riot
Creations

Riot

YOU NEVER
KNOW SOME
THINGS ARE
OUT OF OUR
CONTROL.
RIDE THE
WAVES OF
LIFE!

holy

TORPEDO
EMPIRE

RiotCreations (GER) www.riotcreations.com

aer (TW) www.flickr.com/photos/cotton120

Sabrina Müller (GER) www.sabrinamueller.com

stefanie axmann (GER) www.stefanieaxmann.com

Anne Rüter (GER) www.neoterisch.com

Dennis Schuster (GER) www.flickr.com/photos/dxtrs

accessoires

handbags, pillows, caps
wallets, shoes, hats

David Crla (CZE) davidcrla.com

David Crla (CZE) davidcrla.com

easy
DOES IT

Fiorella Carla Cambareri (ARG) fiocamba_512@hotmail.com

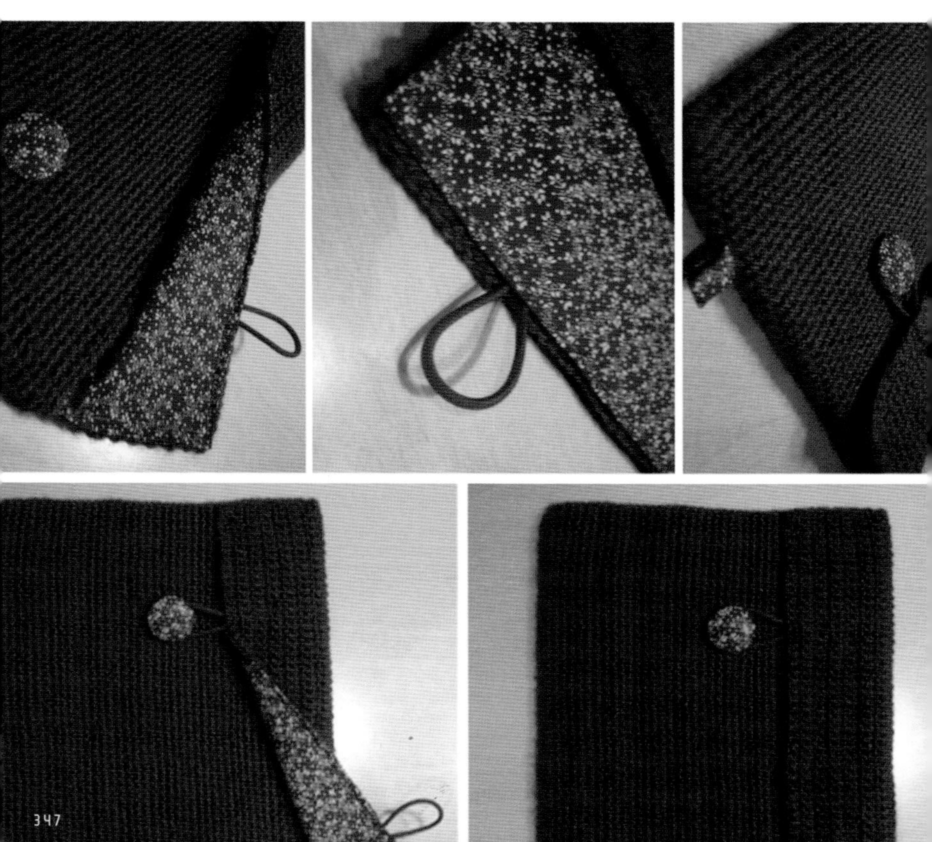

Thomas Frederiksen & Jakob Fuglsang (DEN) www.shoethebear.com

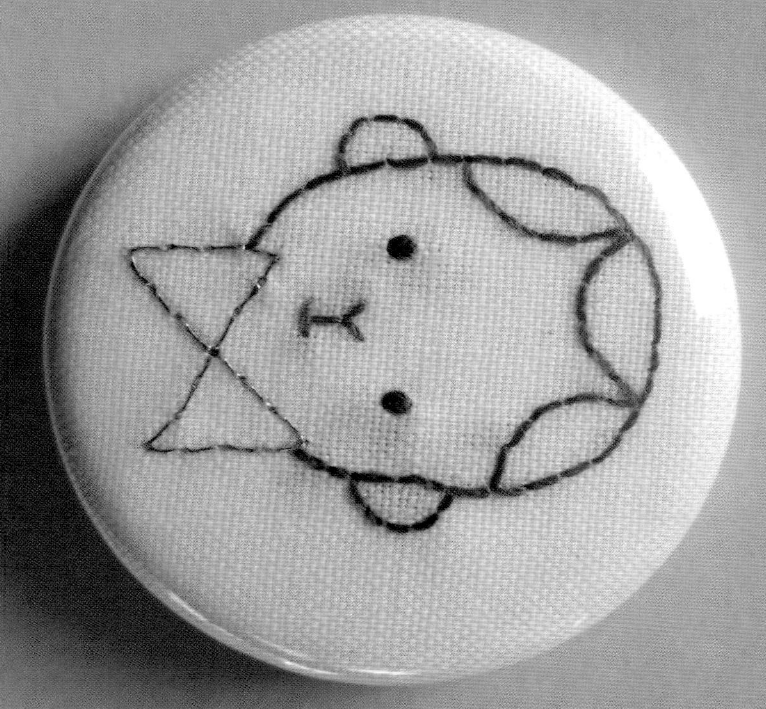

 Audrey Jeanne (FRA) www.audreyjeanne.blogspot.com

Audrey Jeanne (FRA) www.audreyjeanne.blogspot.com

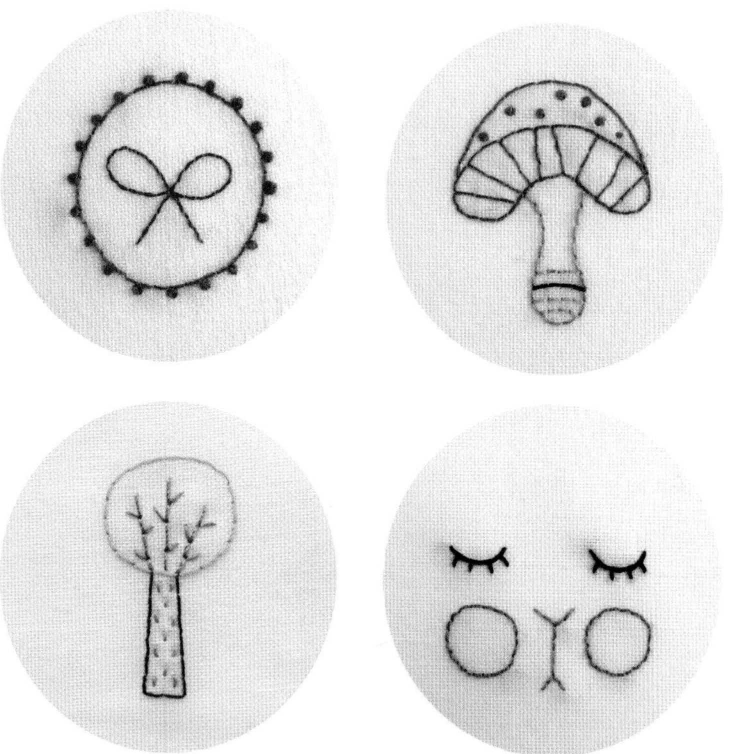

smil

Nadja Girod (GER) www.nadjagirod.com

Nadja Girod (GER) www.nadjagirod.com

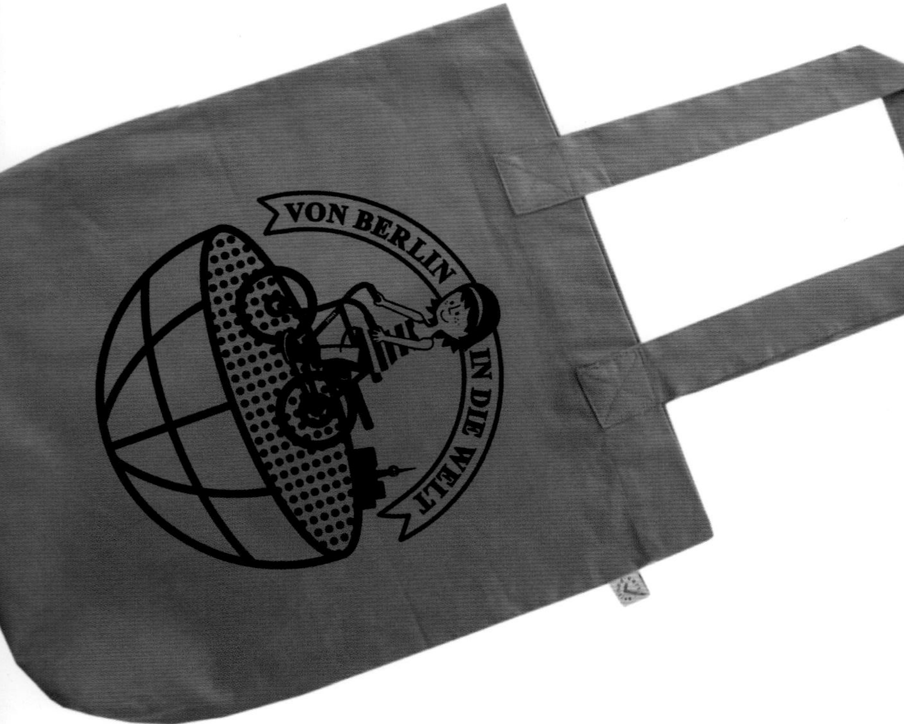
VON BERLIN
IN DIE WELT

VON BERLIN
IN DIE WELT

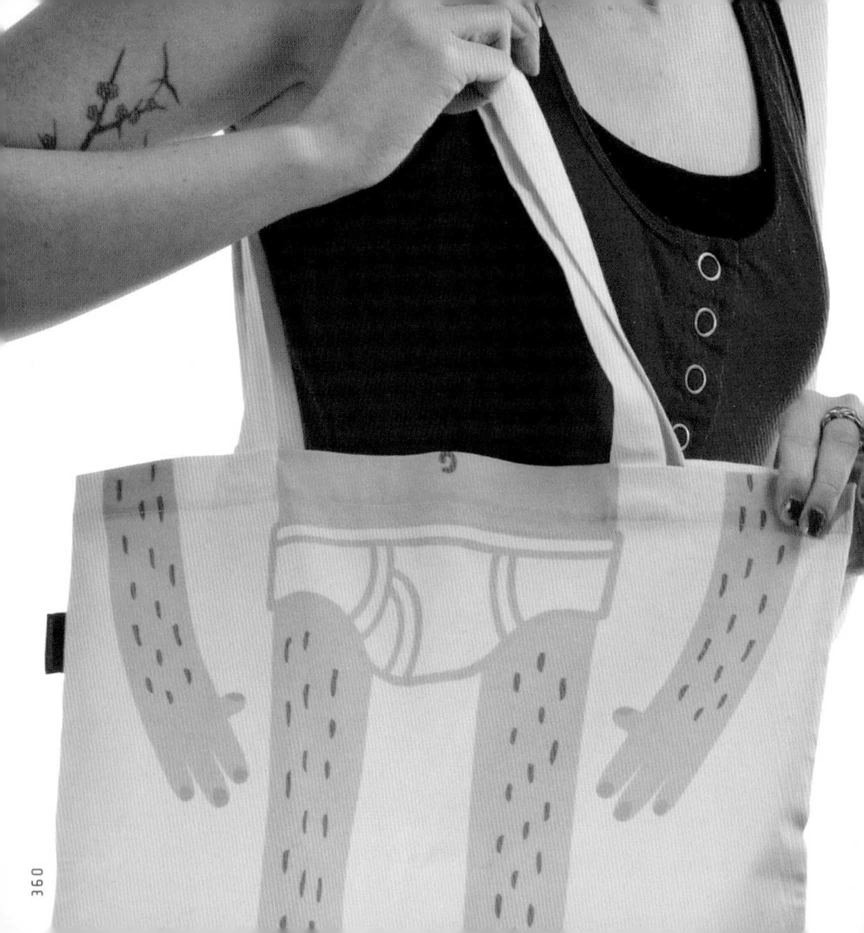

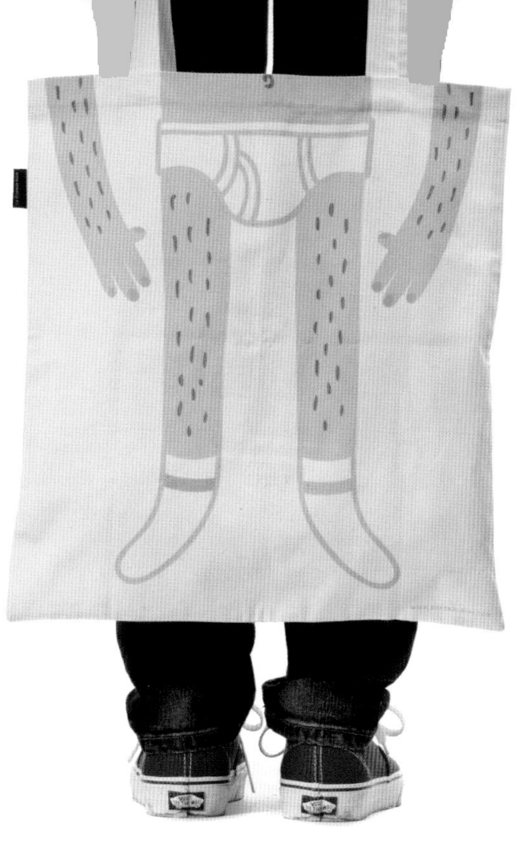

Bart Aalbers [NED] www.bartaalbers.com

Nadya Petrova (RUS) www.flickr.com/p...sheepdeer

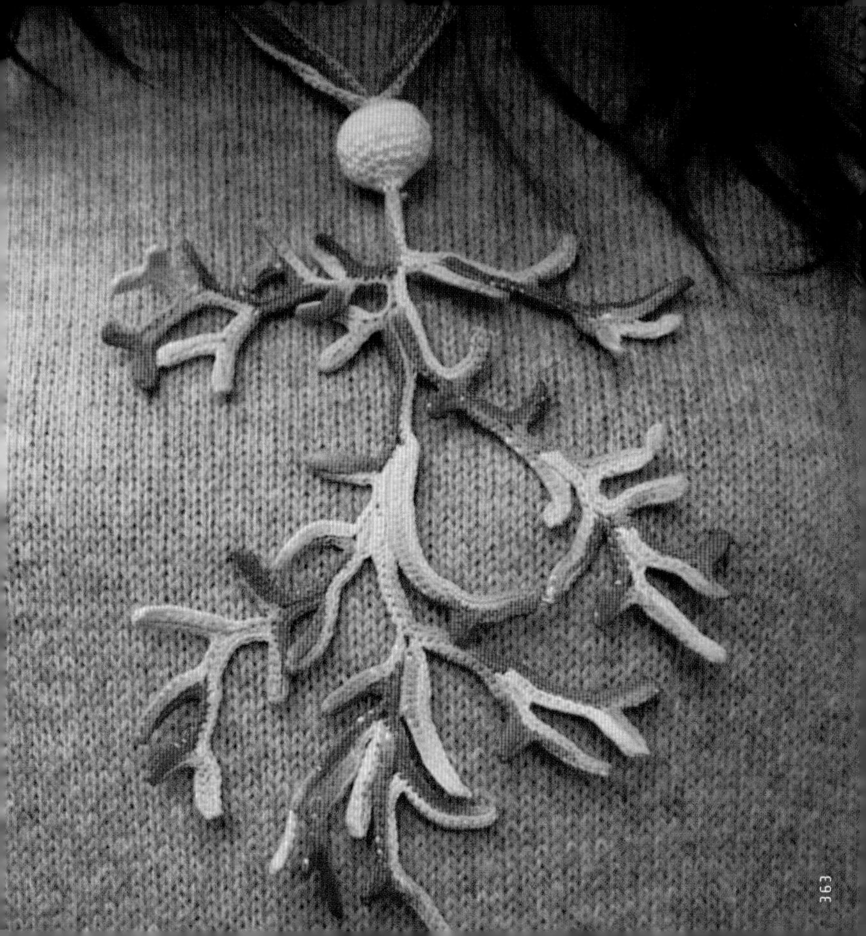

Nadja Girod (GER) www.nadjagirod.com

AHOI

19.9.
FREITAG
2008
DJ's
Soliparty
WIRR
EASYEMRE
33 funk
MARIO SCHOO & MOK
MBF
SPECTRAL
CONNAISSEUR
Live Acts:
VJING!
Graffiti
CREDENZA
MC BASTI
CHOONTZI
DWW
EINTRITT:
5€
Special GUESTS
IM
AZ
LIEBIGSTR.29
OSNABRÜCK
NEUE GESICHTER

Galtsova Irina (RUS) irina.galtsova@gmail.ru

Anne Dietrich (GDR) contact@hatgirl.de

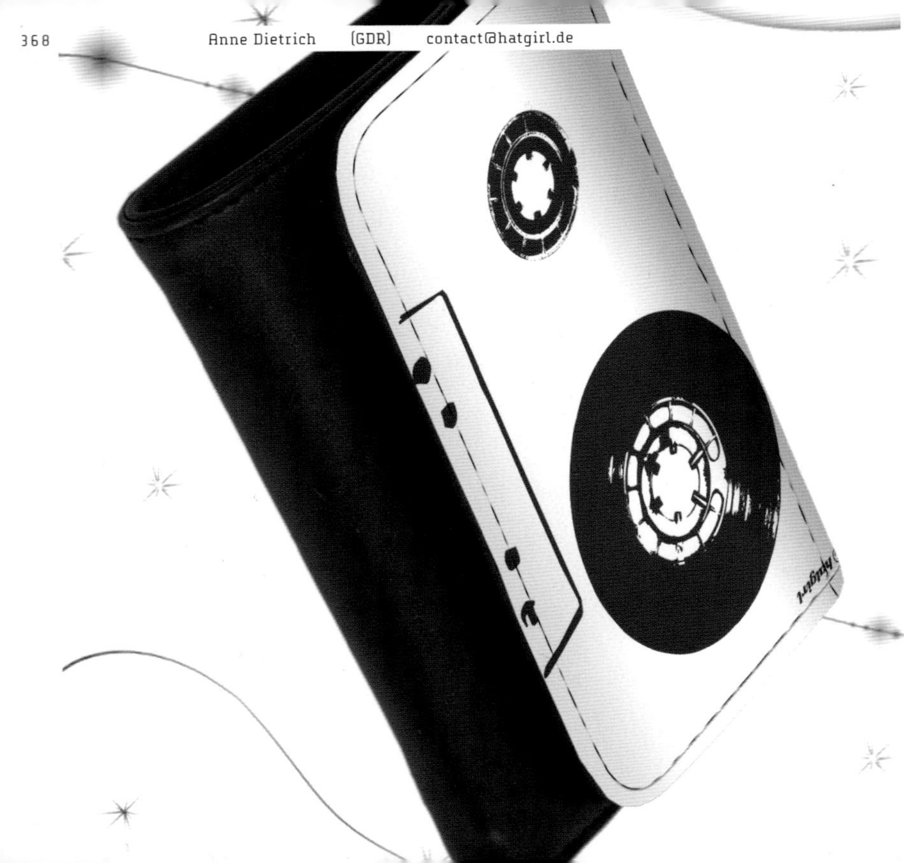

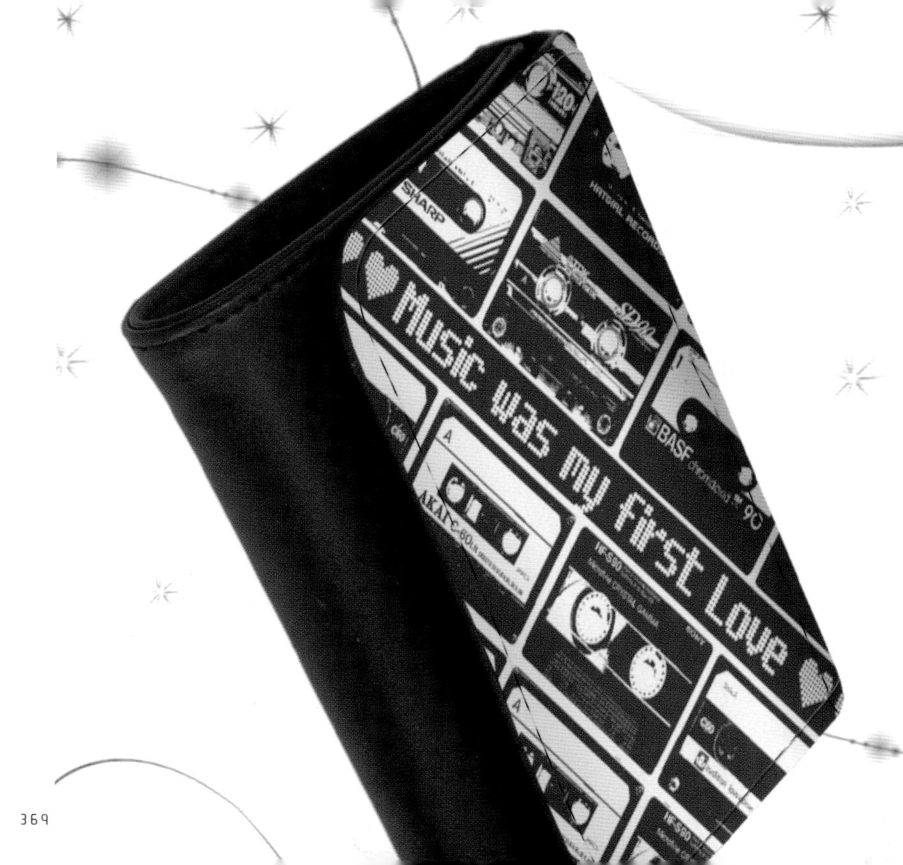
Music was my first Love
SHARP
BASF
AKAI

Anne Dietrich (GDR) contact@hatgirl.de

Anukun Hamala (THA) www.nokhookdesign.com

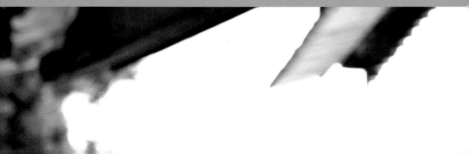

Anukun Hamala (THA) www.nokhookdesign.com

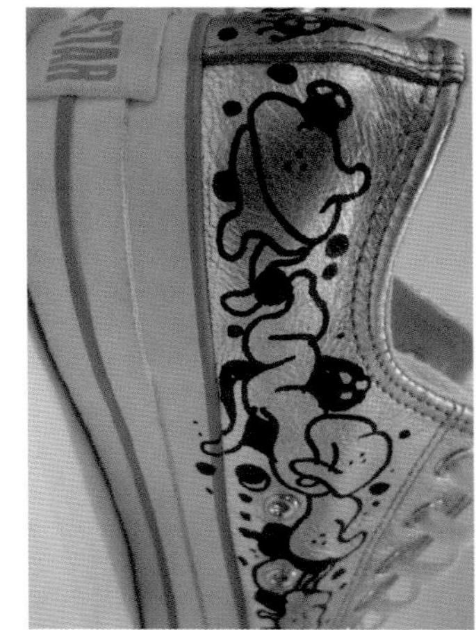

Anukun Hamala (THA) www.nokhookdesign.com

Josephine Kimberling (USA) www.josephinekimberling.com

Audrey Jeanne (FRA) www.audreyjeanne.blogspot.com

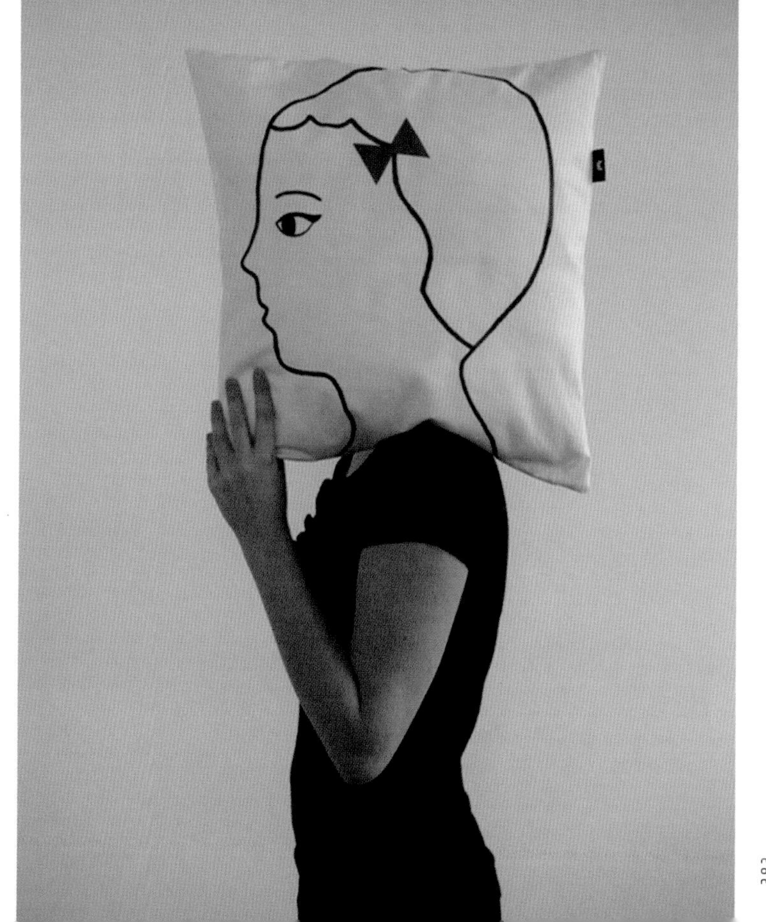

Audrey Jeanne (FRA) www.audreyjeanne.blogspot.com

 Audrey Jeanne (FRA) www.audreyjeanne.blogspot.com

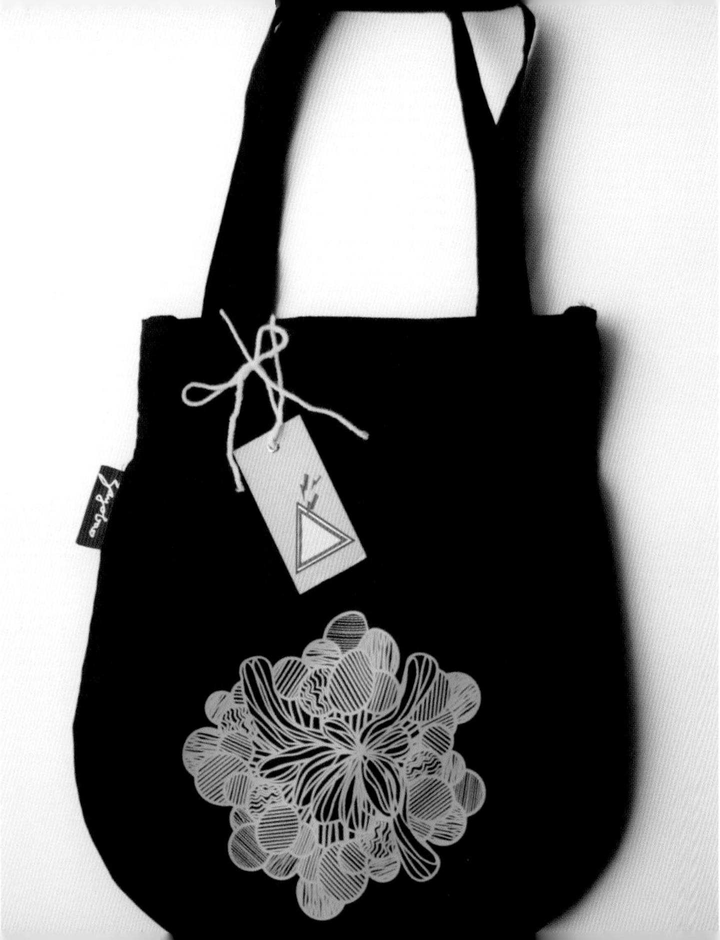

zayoba (GER) www.zayoba.de

tanja devetak (SLO) www.suanaverelst.com

Suana Verelst (CAN) www.suanaverelst.com

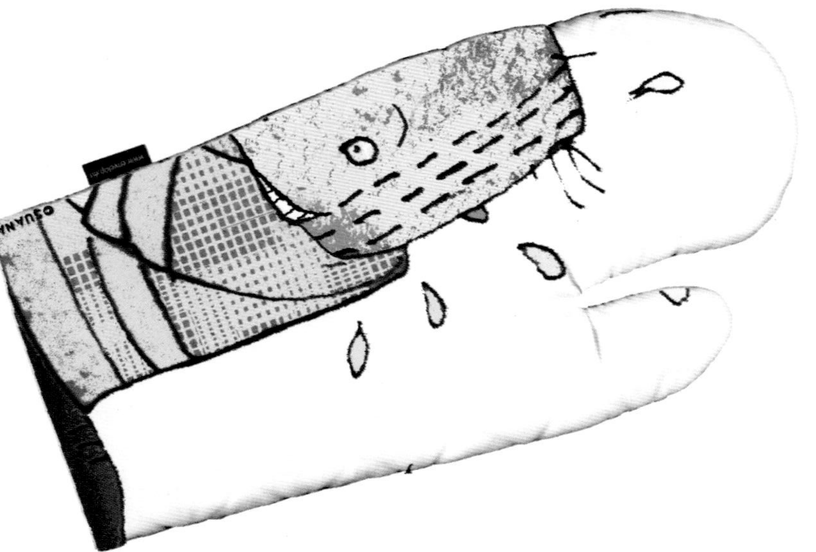

©SUANA

Mariano Ledwith (ARG) www. www.flickr.com/photos/soygroso

Alicia Villodres (ESP) www. alicia-villodres.blogspot.com

Laura Hoyer (USA) www.openfacesandwich.com

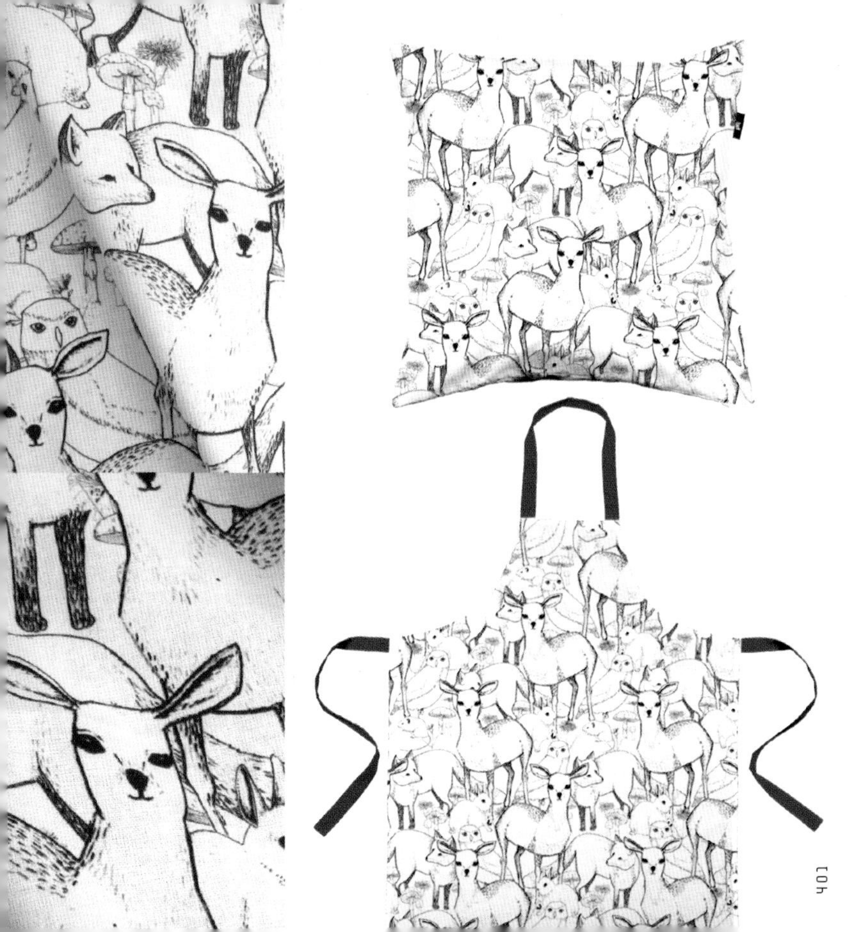

jag
älskar di
je t'aime
я тебя люблю
te amo
ich liebe
dich
我爱你
i love
you

jag
älskar di
je t'aime
я тебя люблю
te amo
ich liebe
dich
我爱你
i love
you

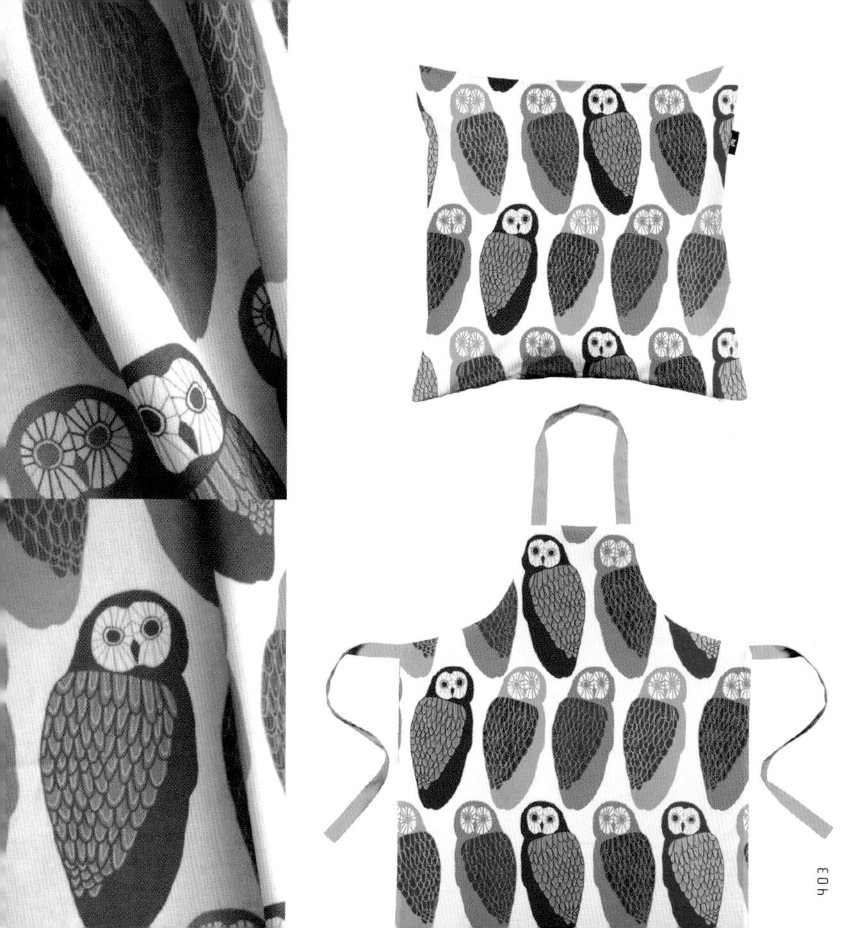

Kama (INA) www.oxidizzy.com

Monica Greco

www.envelop.eu/shop/monica-greco

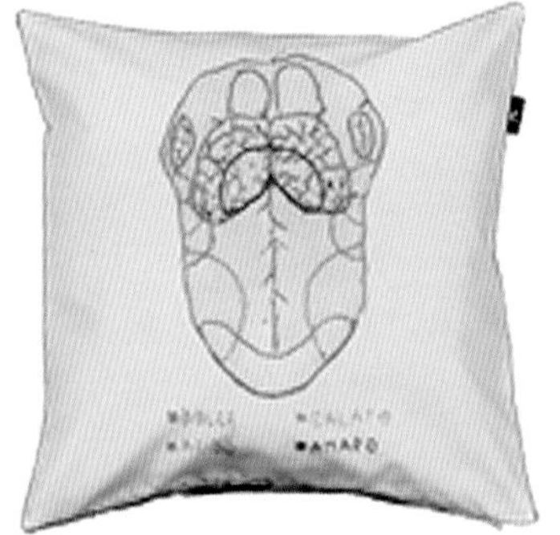

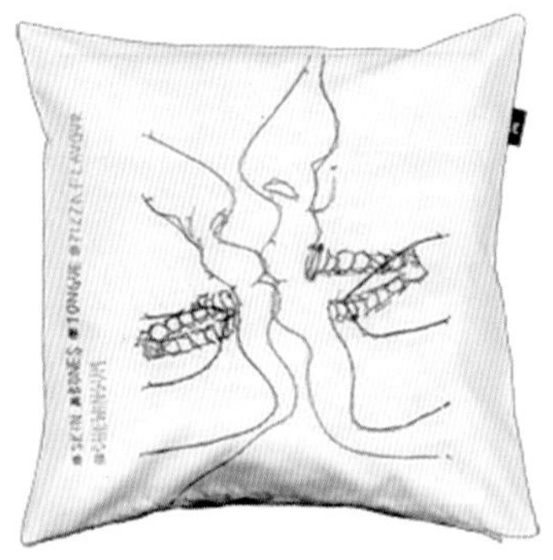

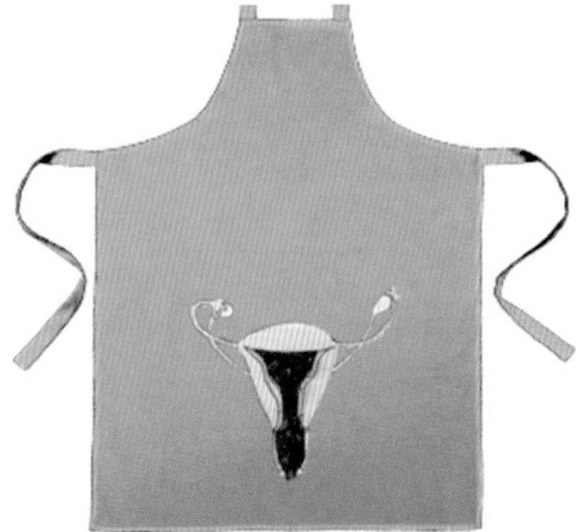

10am (GRE) myspace.com/10antemeridiem

Jenni Tuominen (FIN) www.sorsapukki.fi

what HAS stripes AND is BLACK AND white?
Musa

Lara Brehm (FRA) www.larabrehm.blogspot.com

isn't it a lovely day to be caught in the rain?
isn't it a lovely day to be caught in the rain?
isn't it a lovely day to be caught in the rain?
isn't it a lovely day to be caught in the rain?
isn't it a lovely day to be caught in the rain?
isn't it a lovely day to be caught in the rain?

Nadja Girod (GER) www.nadjagirod.com

Galtsova Irina (RUS) irina.galtsova@gmail.ru

Galtsova Irina (RUS) irina.galtsova@gmail.ru

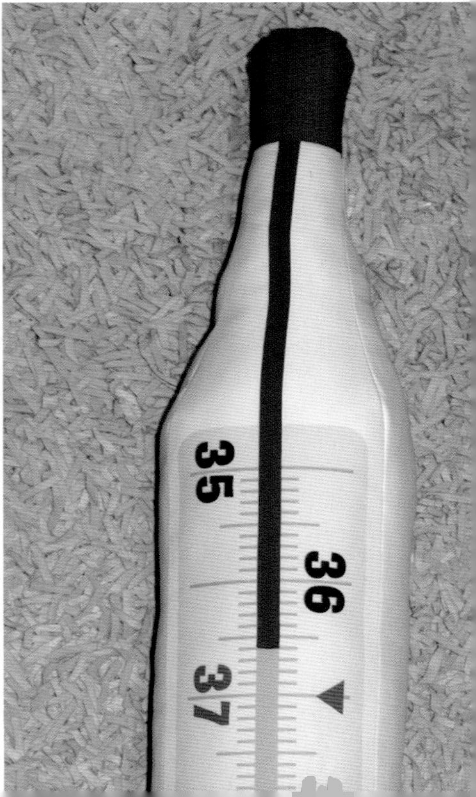

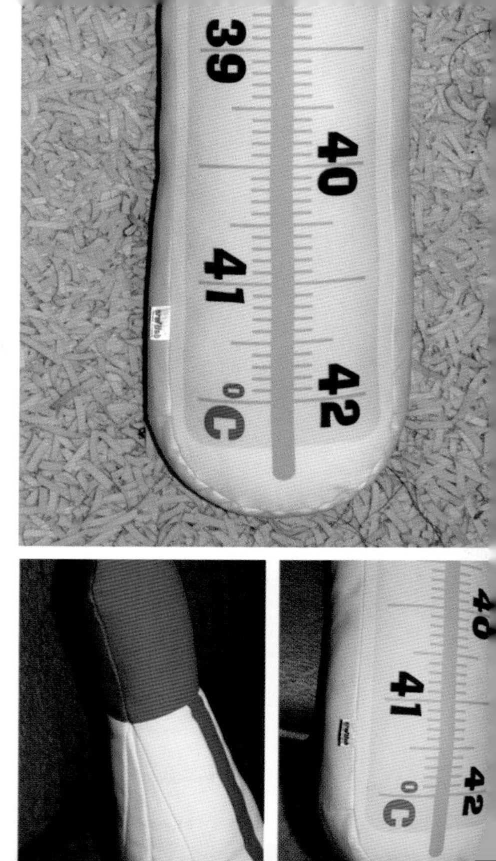
39
40
41
42
°C

Thomas Dabner (GBR) www.fivesandzeros.blogspot.com

Nozzle check shows low cyan ink level
PGBK

Nozzle check shows low black ink level
PGBK
C
C
M
M
Y

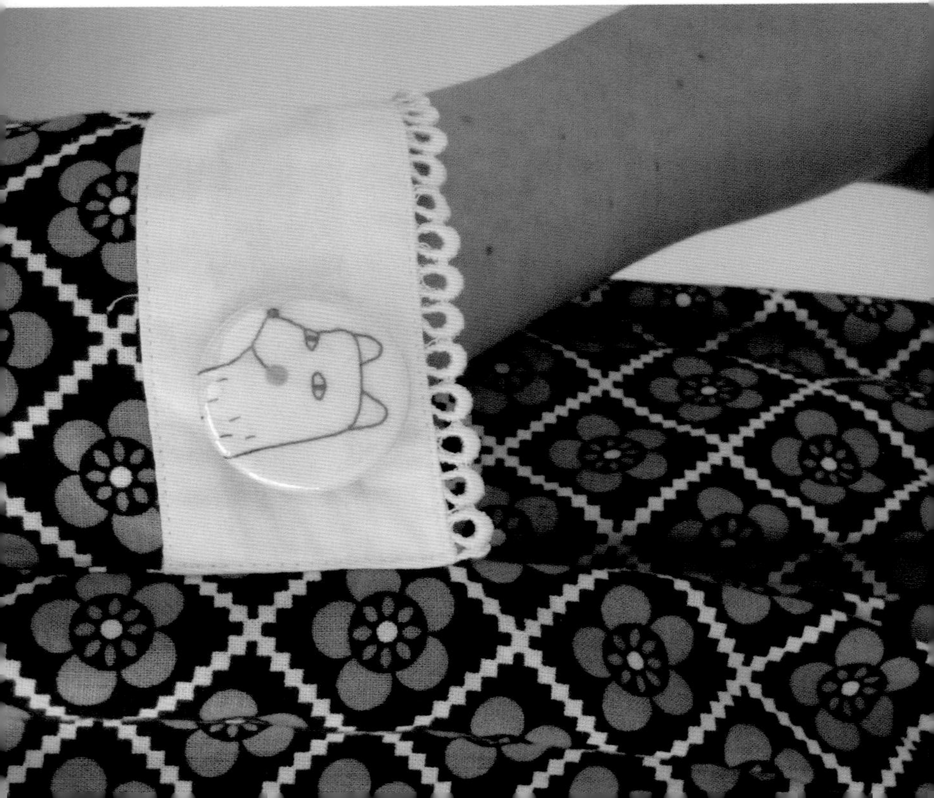

Audrey Jeanne (FRA) www.audreyjeanne.blogspot.com

B
E
A
R
audreyjeanne
Badge en tissu brodé à la main
pièce unique n°0001

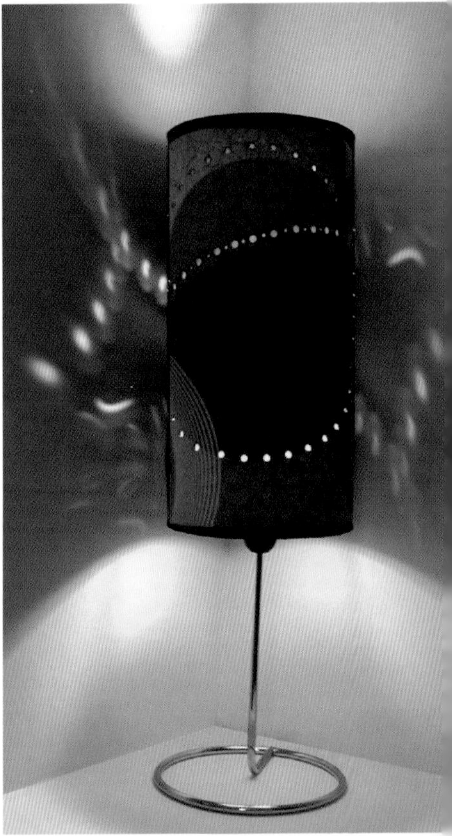

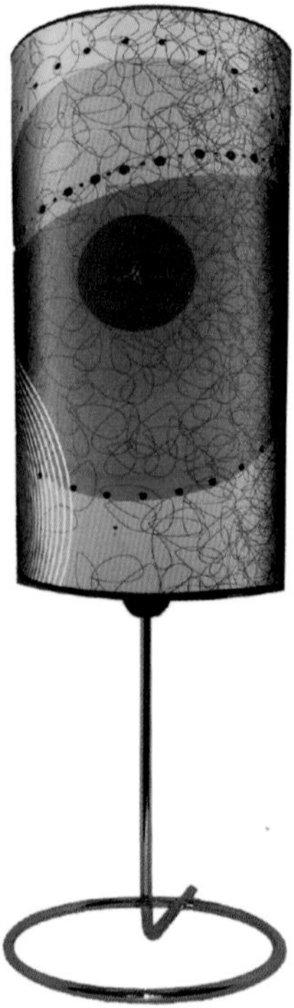

Zeynep Karaca (GBR) www.figgi.net

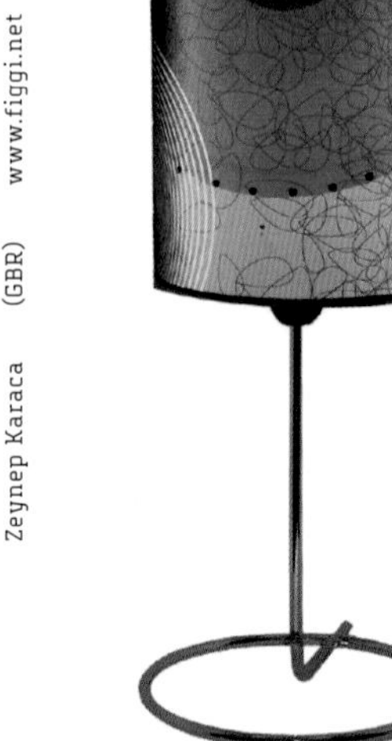

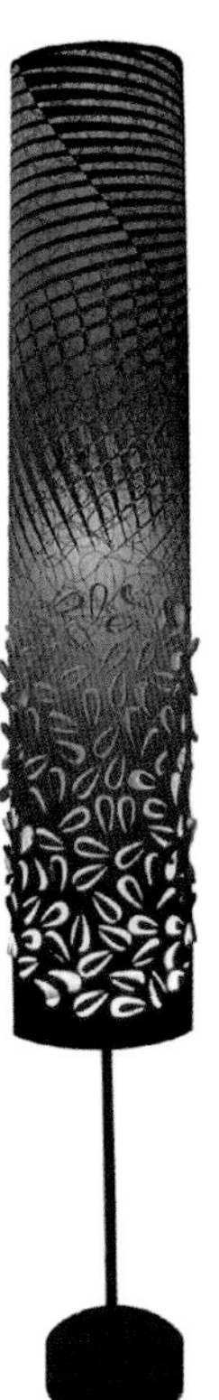

Suz Sanchez (ESP) www.suzsanchez.com

425

Christine Berrie (GBR) www.christineberrie.com

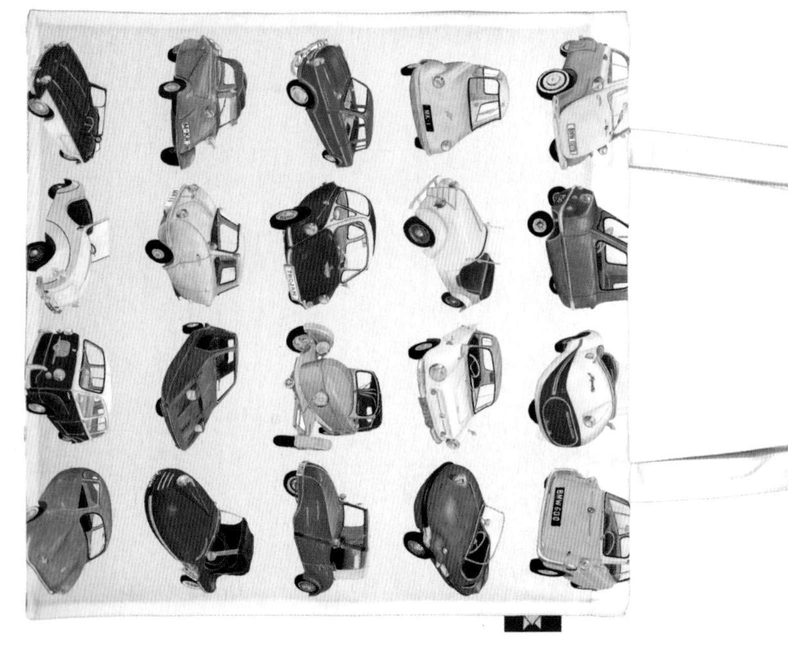

London Bridge
Borough New Cross
Old Kent Road
21
LONDON BRIDGE 21
RM1968

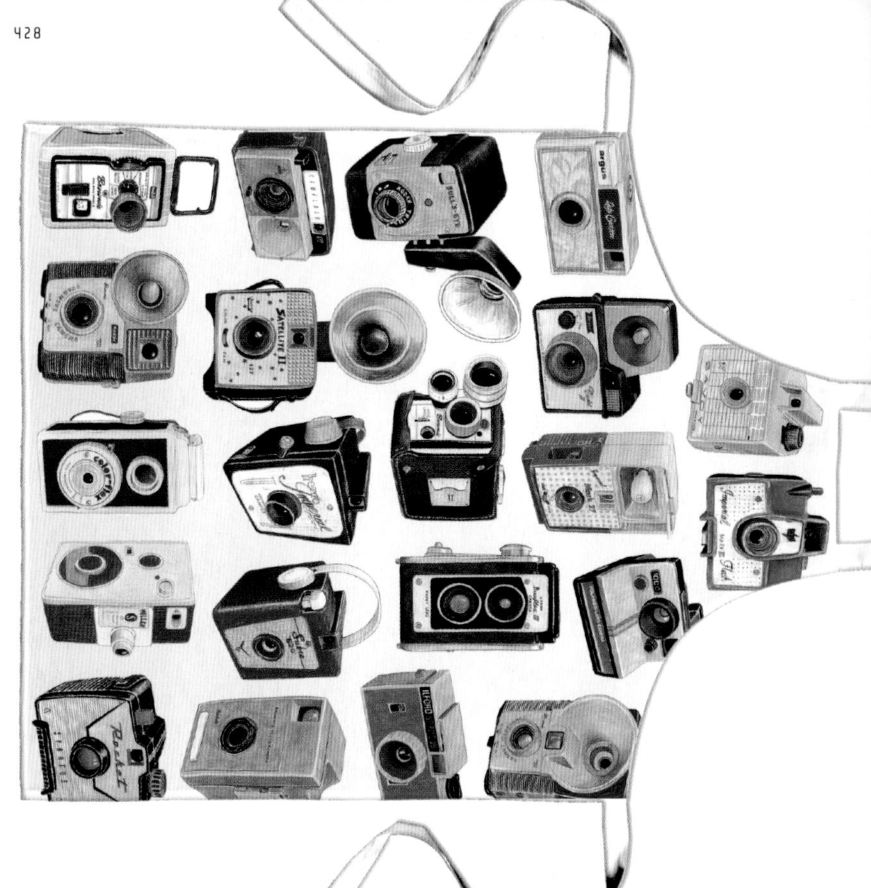
argus
BULL'S-EYE
SATELLITE II
color-flex
Rocket
ILFORD

 Christine Berrie (GBR) www.christineberrie.com

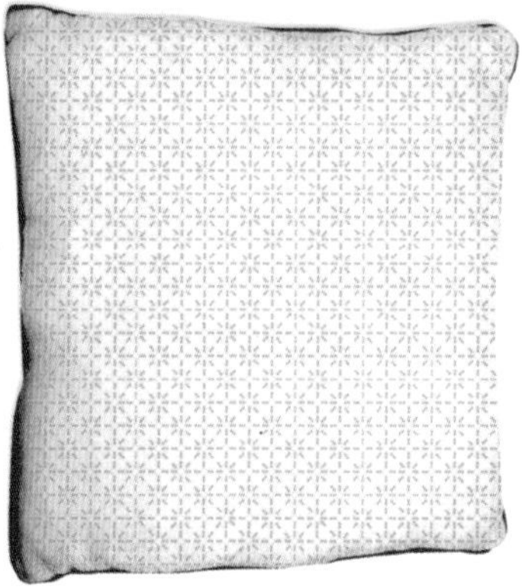

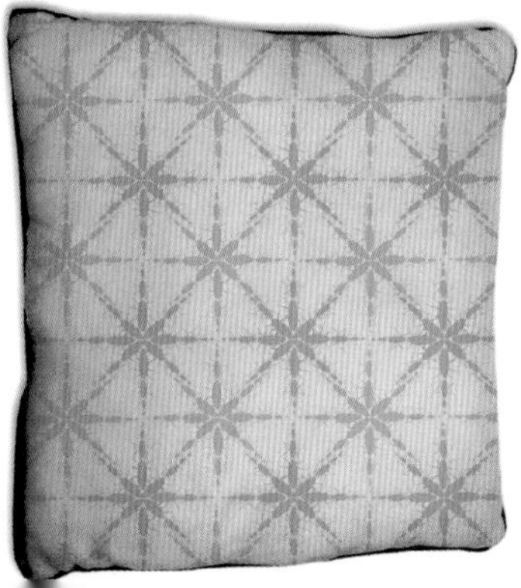

Olivier Arcioli (GER) www.o-j-s.com

Audrey Jeanne (FRA) www.audreyjeanne.blogspot.com

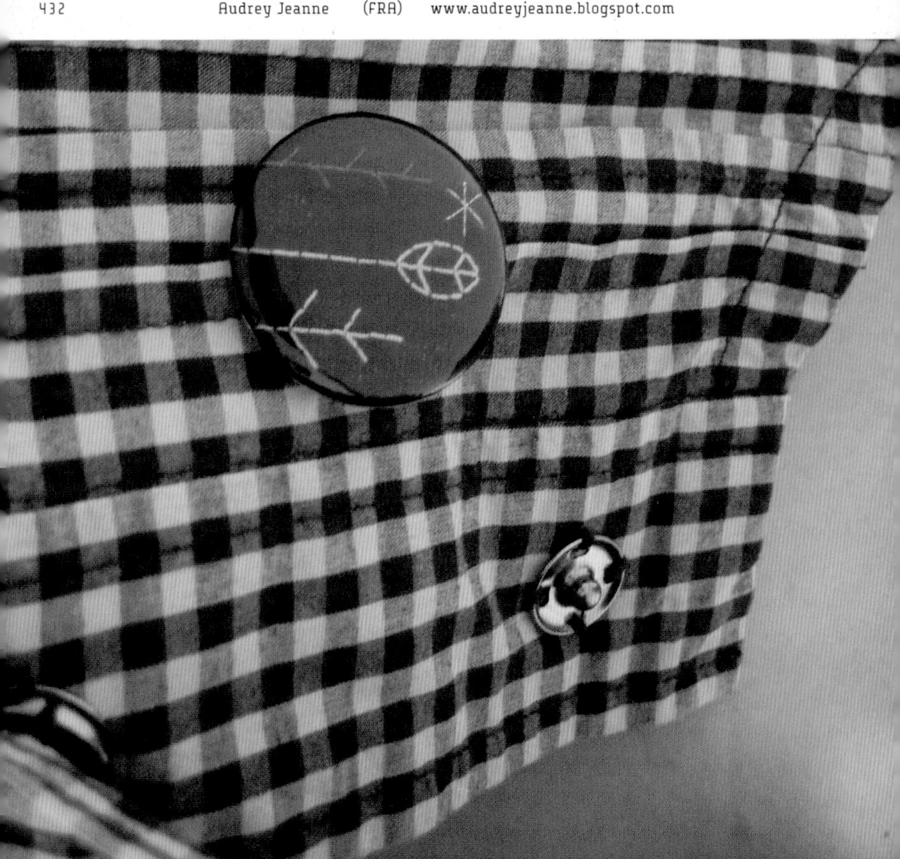

Ulrike Kunkel (GER) www.ritapita.de

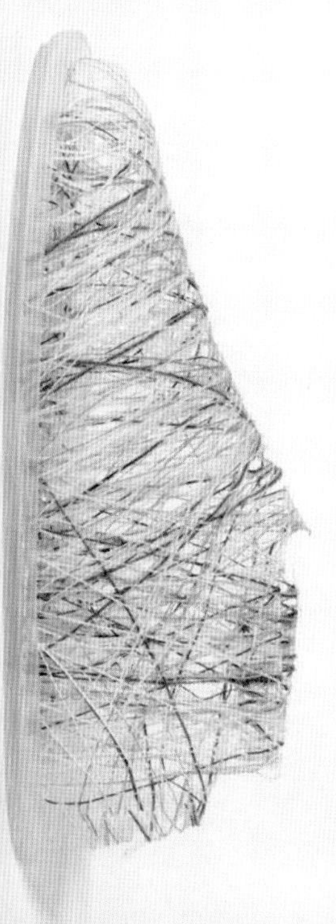

Patricia Yasmine Graf (GER) www.pyg-design.de

Patricia Yasmine Graf (GER) www.pyg-design.de

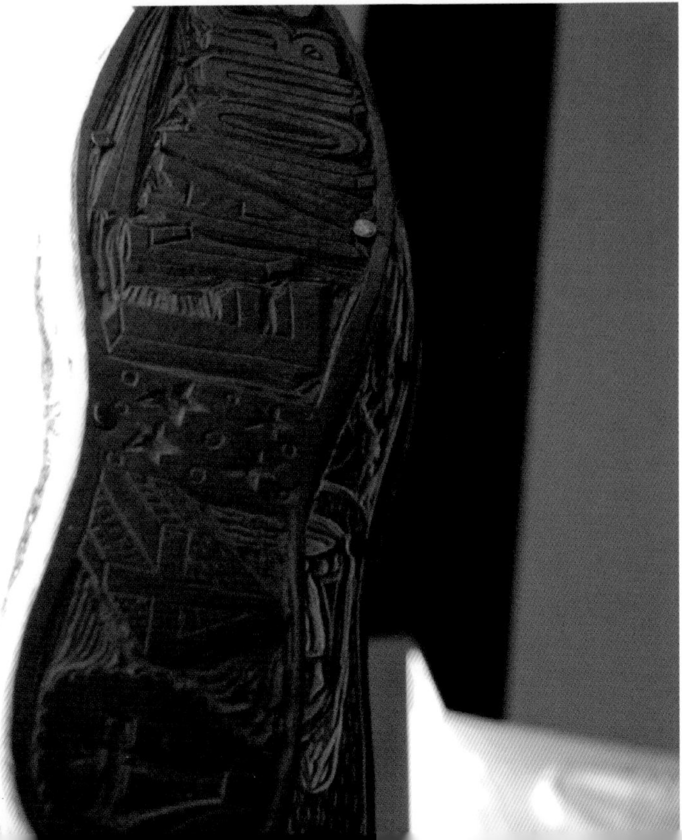

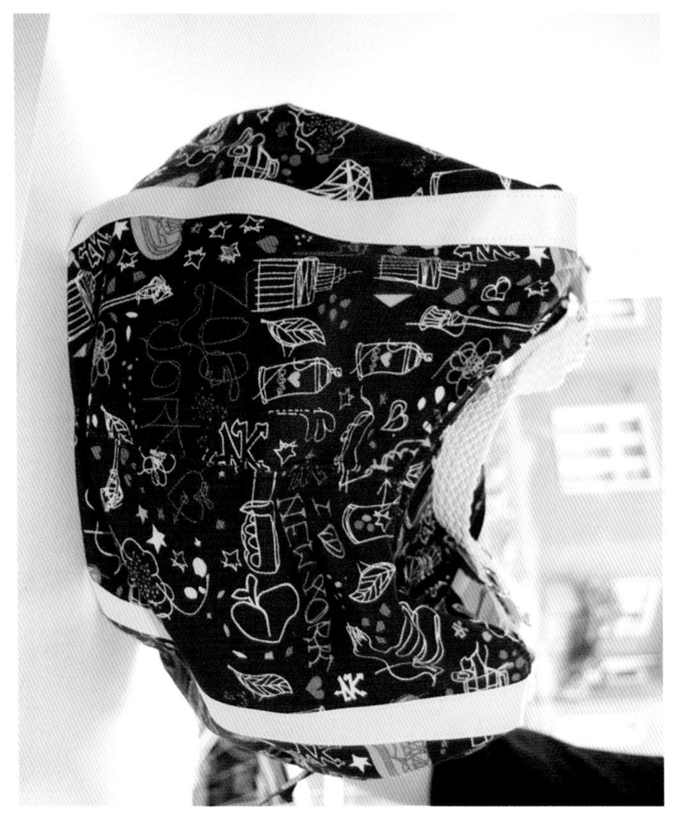

 Julio Rölle (GER) www.44flavours.de

Marie Blanchard (FRA) www.marieblanchard.com

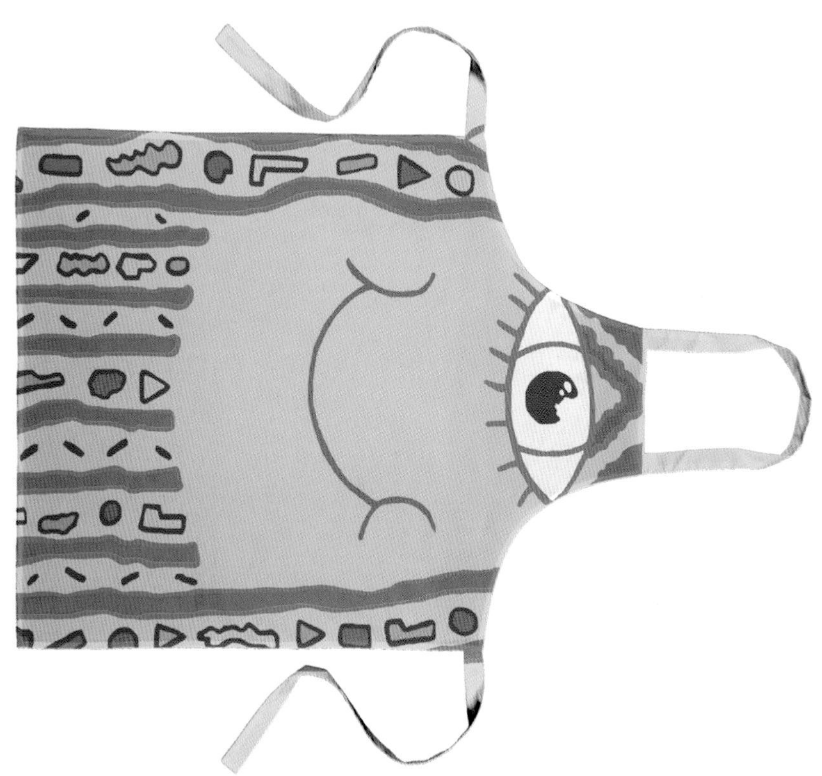

Lorella Pierdicca (ITA) www.lldesign.it

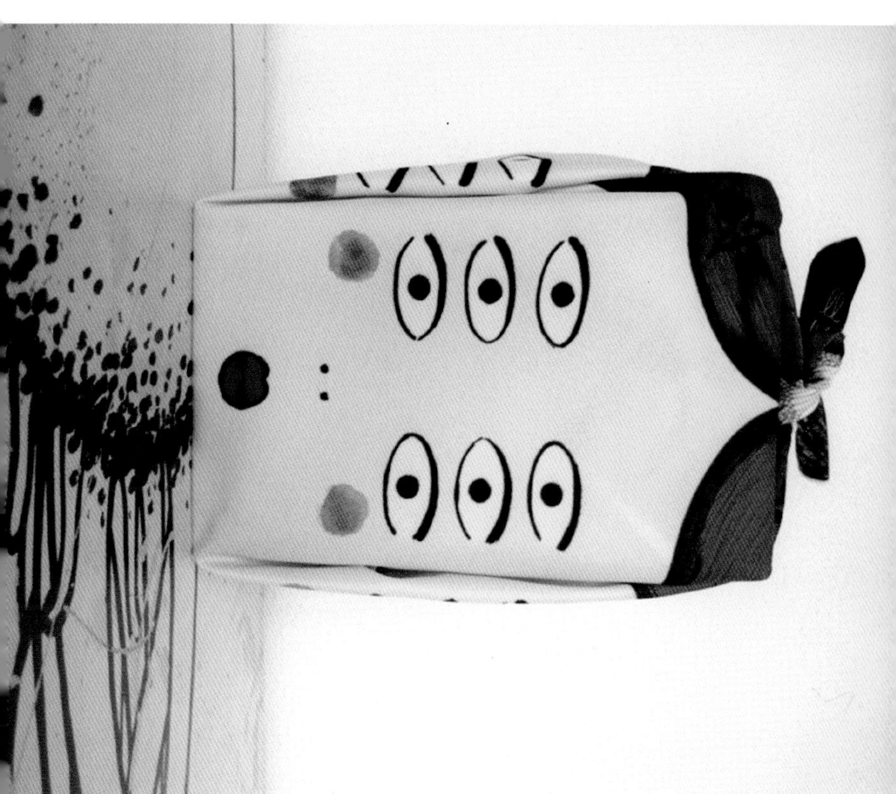

Lorella Pierdicca (ITA) www.lldesign.it

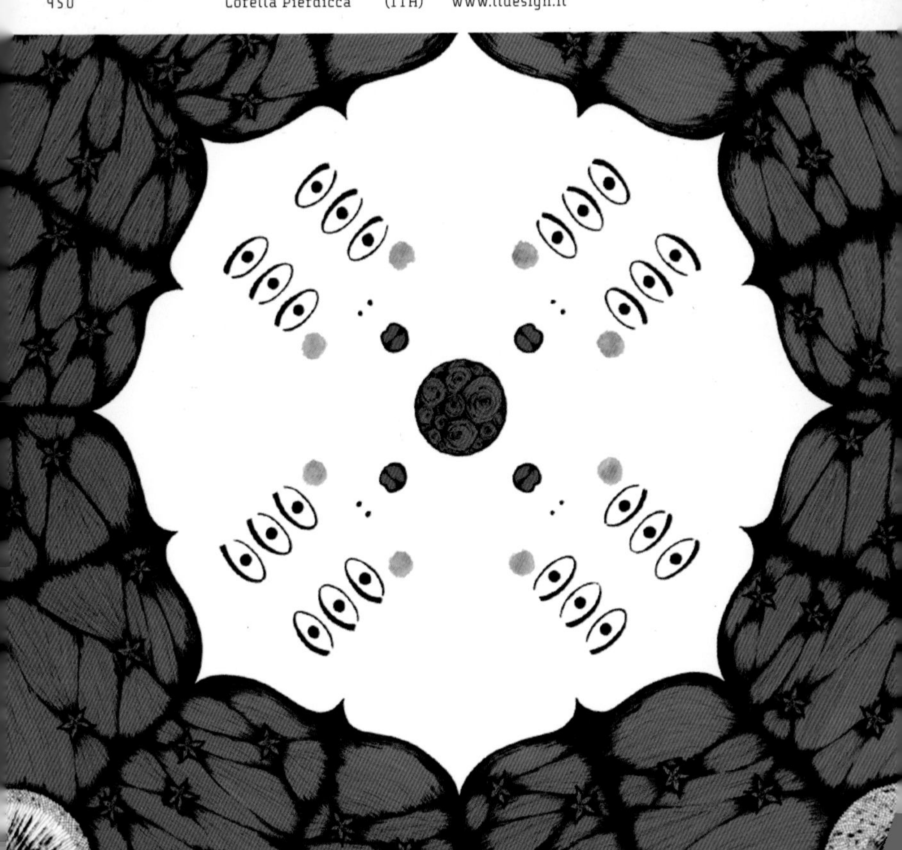

Anne Dietrich (GER) contact@hatgirl.de

Von Glitschka (USA) www.vonglitschka.com

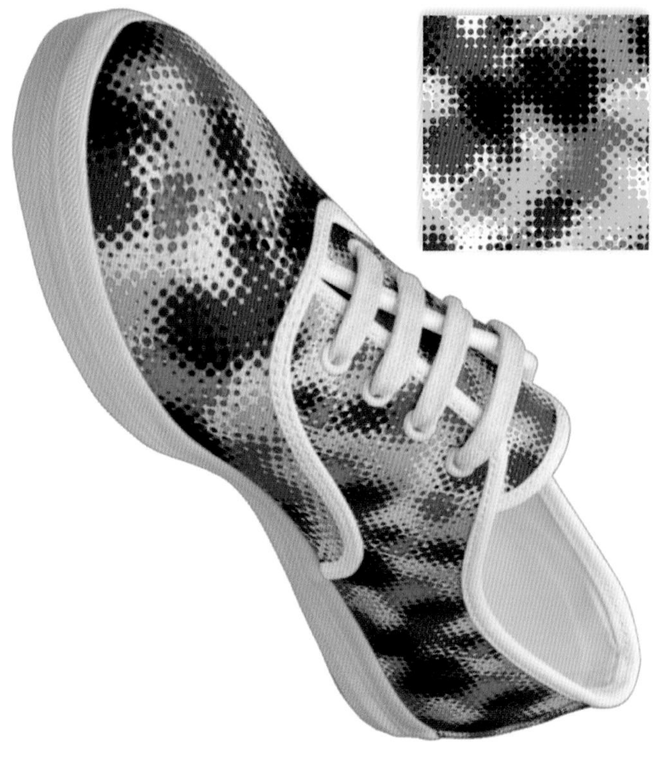

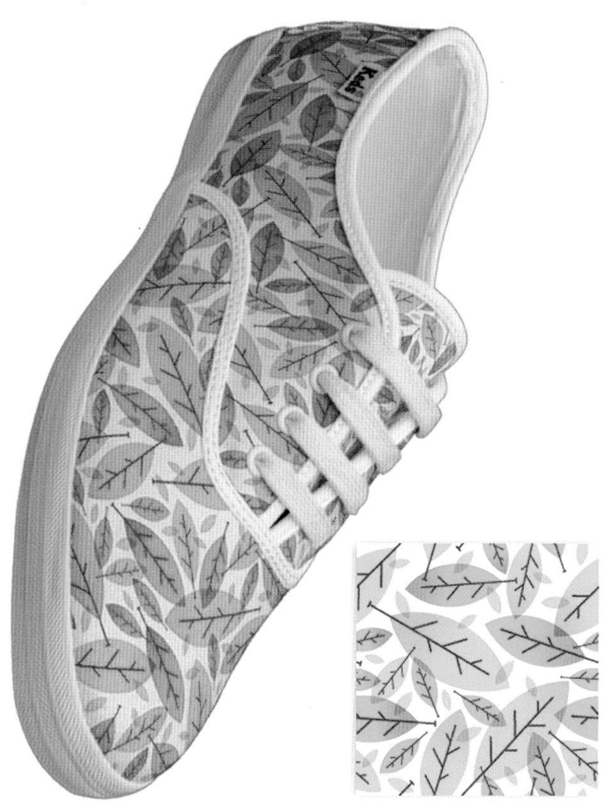
Keds

 Kristina Markovic (GER) www.kristinamarkovic.com

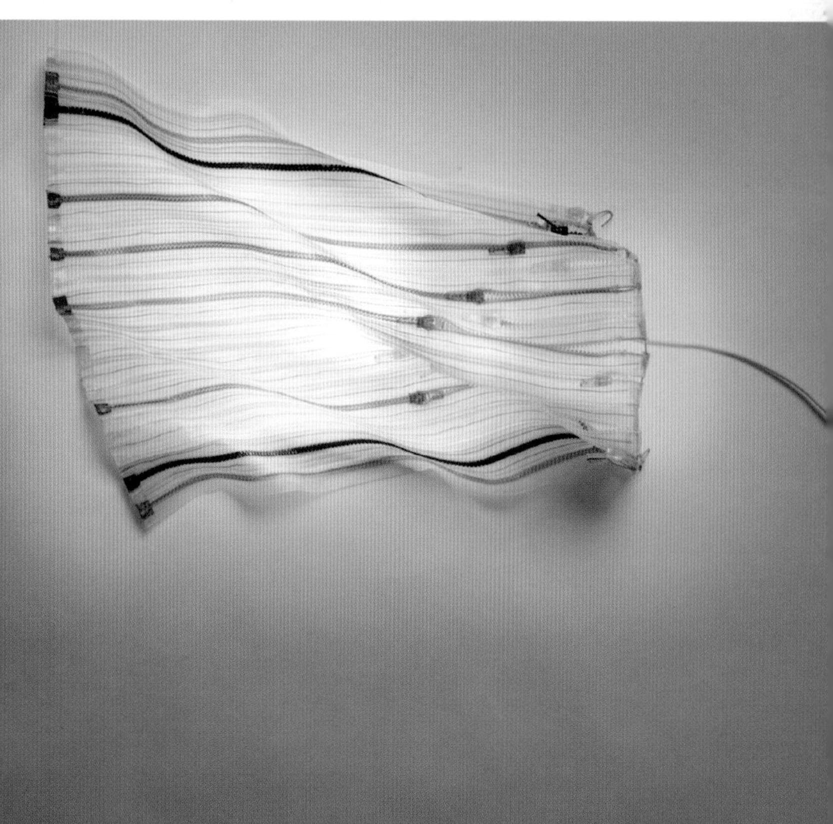

10am (GRE) www.myspace.com/10antemeridiem

www.envelop.eu

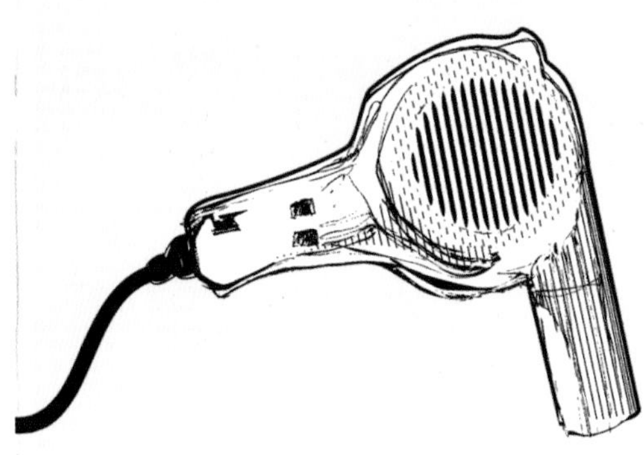

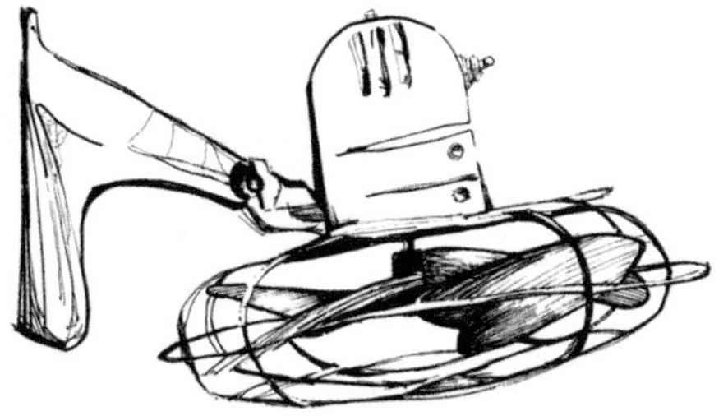

Bart Aalbers (NED) www.bartaalbers.com

easy
DOES IT

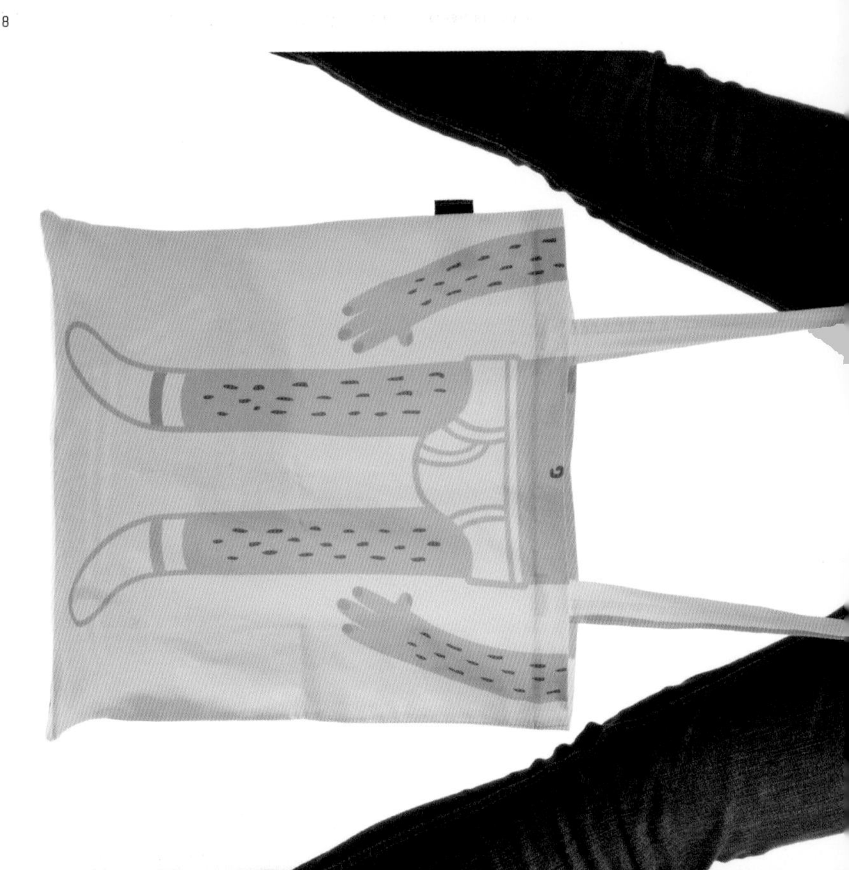

Thomas Dabner (GBR) www.fivesandzeros.blogspot.com

Nozzle check shows low magenta ink level
PGBK
C
C
M
M
Y

Nozzle check shows low yellow ink level

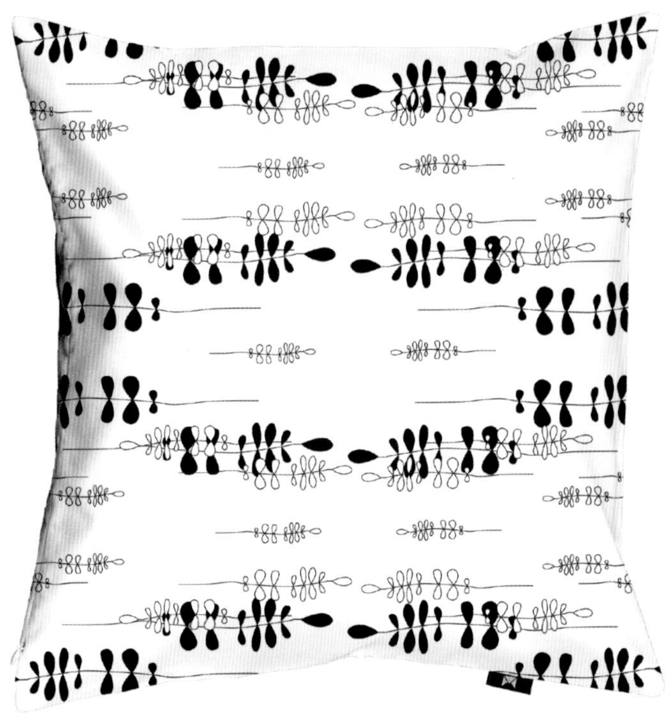

ROYAL

Suz Sanchez (ESP) www.suzsanchez.com

HOME
SWEET
HOME

jelly
jelly
jelly
jelly
Jelly @cm
Jelly @cm

 Eike Mitte (GER) www.vectorian.de

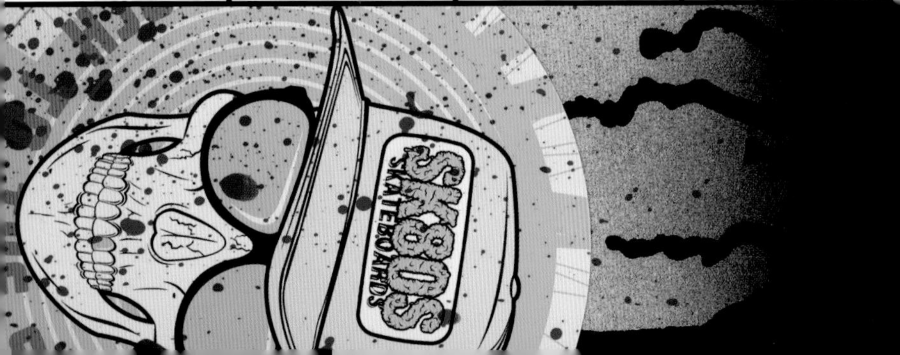

 Florian Mihr (GER) www.sk80s.com

SK80S

SK8OS
SKATEBOARDS
WWW.SK8OS.COM
SK8OS
SKATEBOARDS

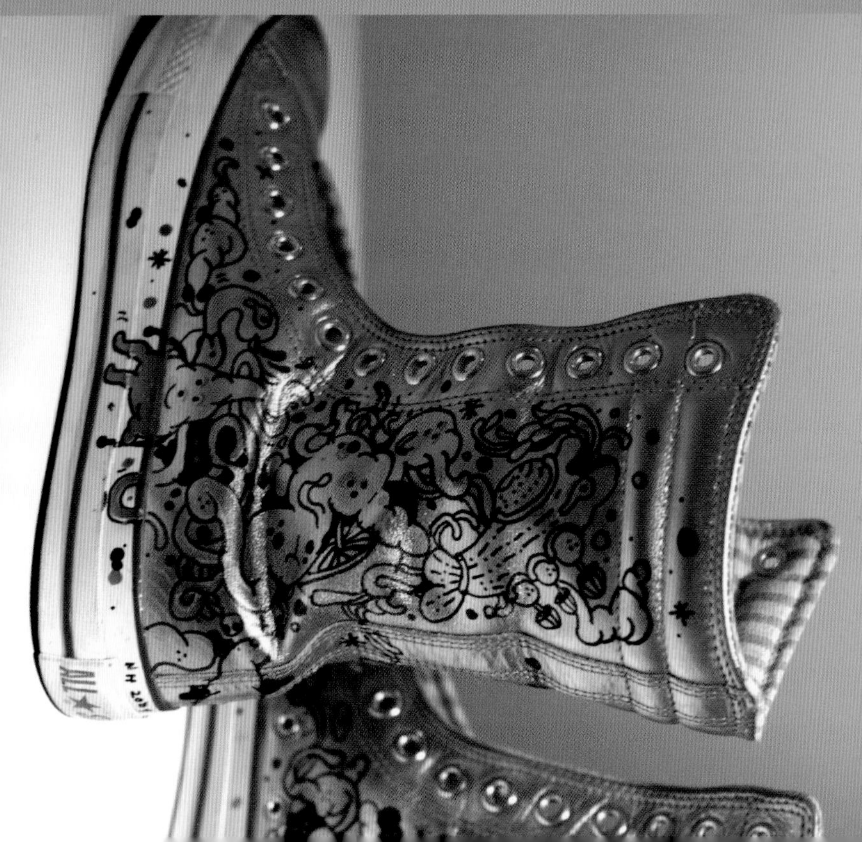

Anukun Hamala (THA) www.nokhookdesign.com

Ulrike Kunkel (GER) www.ritapita.de

Wagner Campelo (BRA) www.wagnercampelo.com

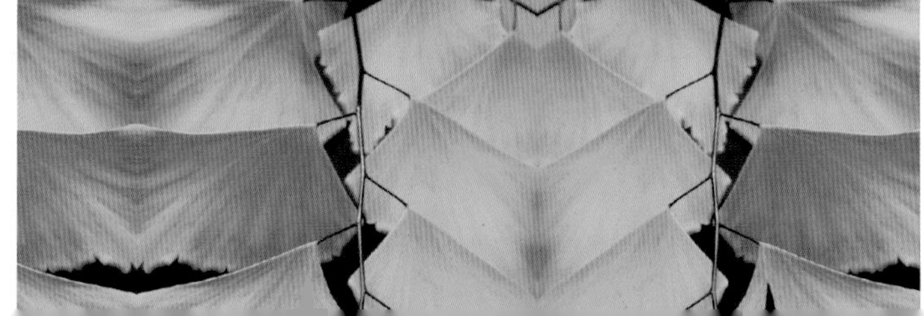

Fiorella Carla Cambareri (ARG) fiocamba_512@hotmail.com

Fiorella Carla Cambareri (ARG) fiocamba_512@hotmail.com

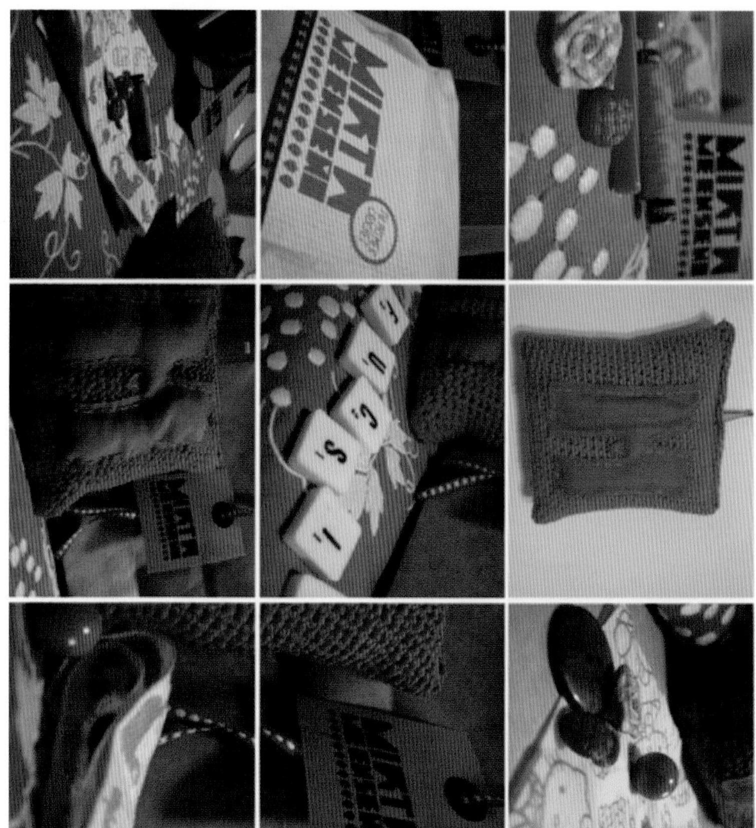

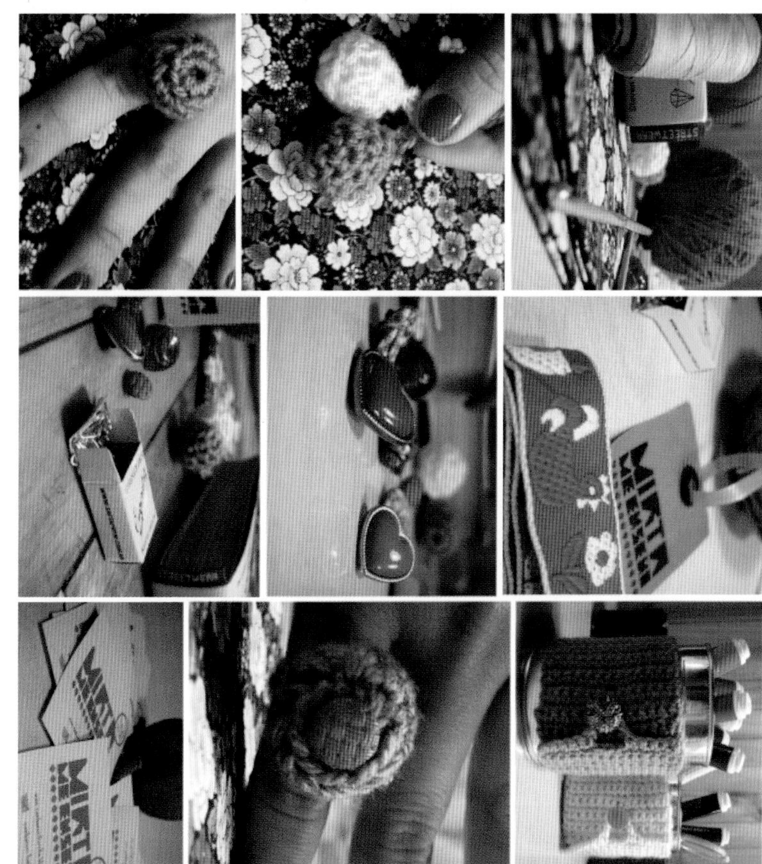

Remona Poortman (NED) www.remona-poortman.blogspot.com

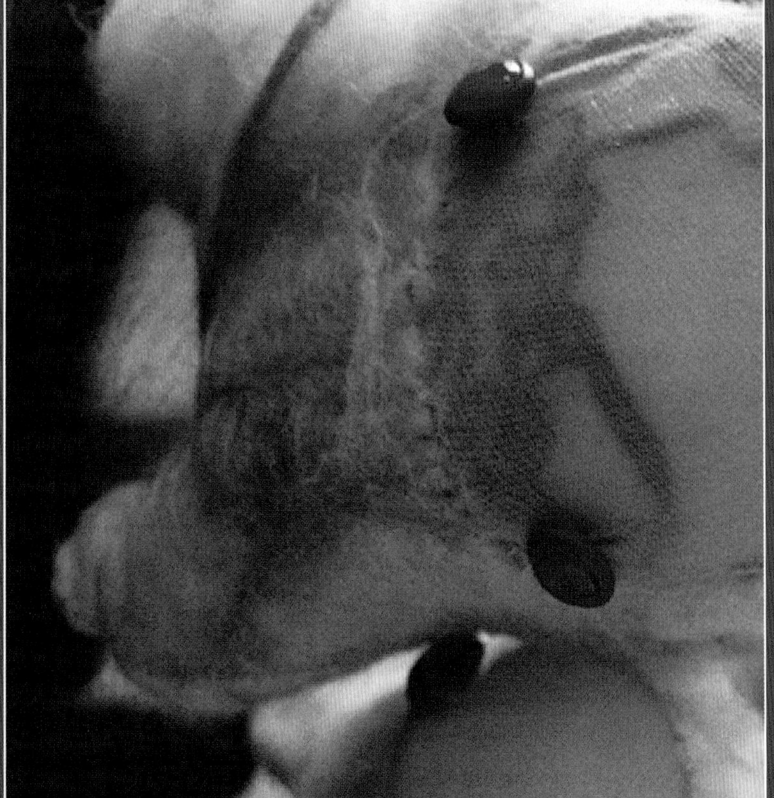

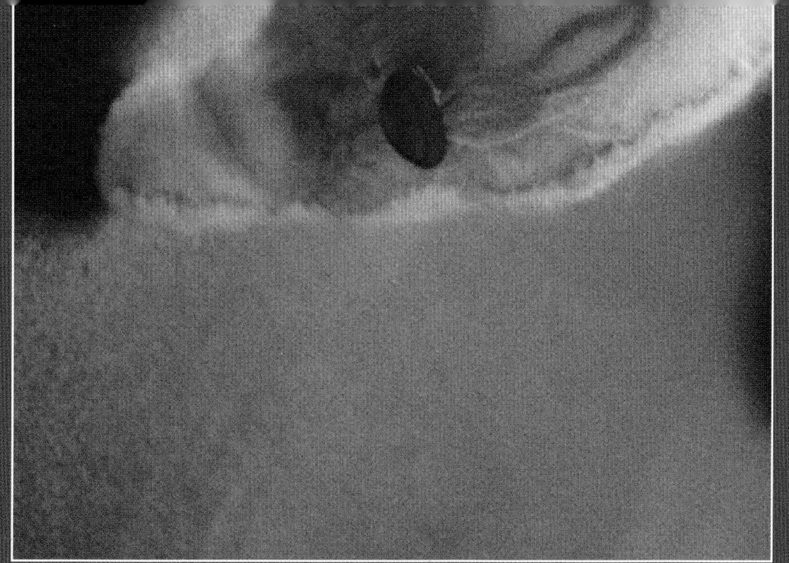

Remona Poortman (NED) www.remona-poortman.blogspot.com

Lloyd Evans (GBR) www.designhousestudios.co.uk

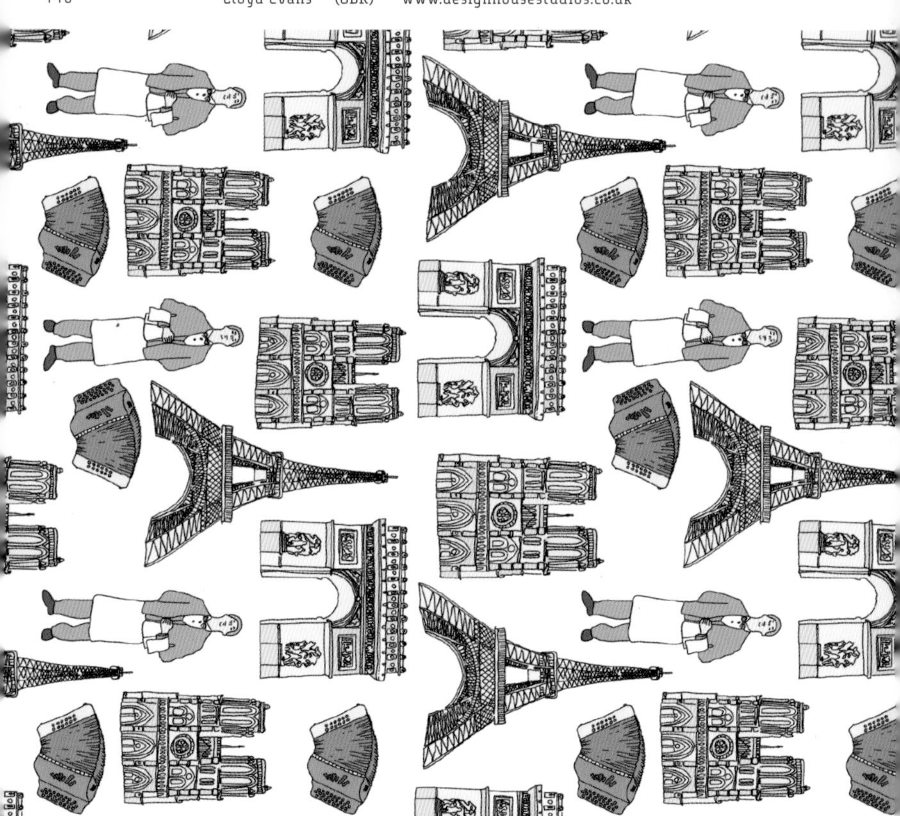

Lloyd Evans (GBR) www.designhousestudios.co.uk

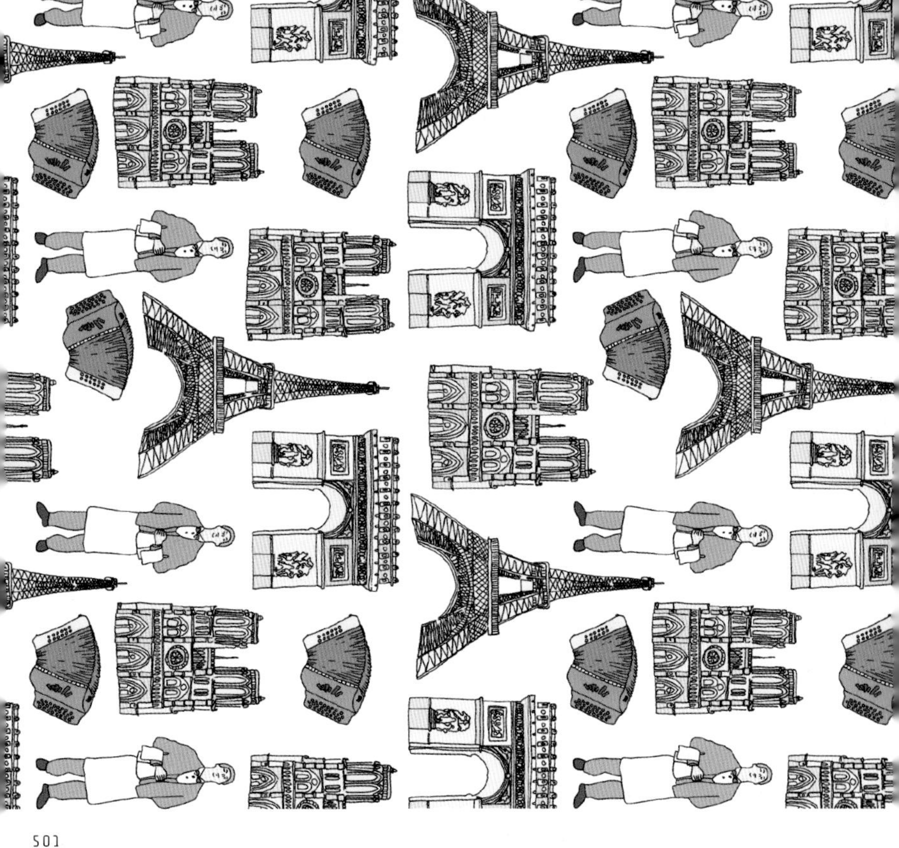

Liebe
ACH**

mag auch ...
BUBEN

Véronique Stohrer (GER) www.veronique-stohrer.com

Véronique Stohrer (GER) www.veronique-stohrer.com

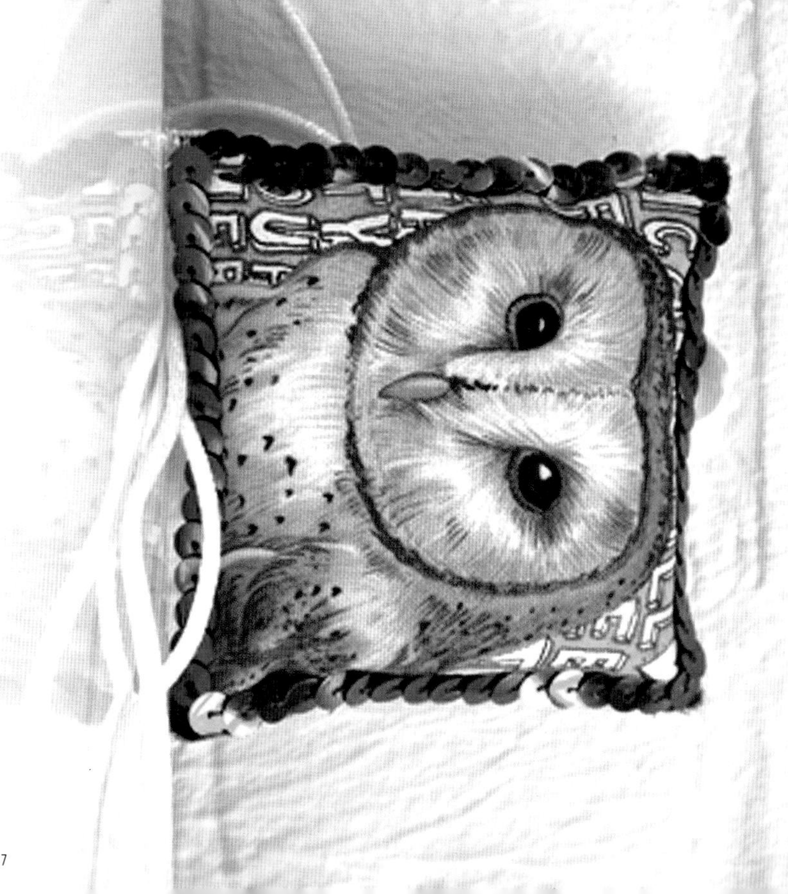

Véronique Stohrer (GER) www.veronique-stohrer.com

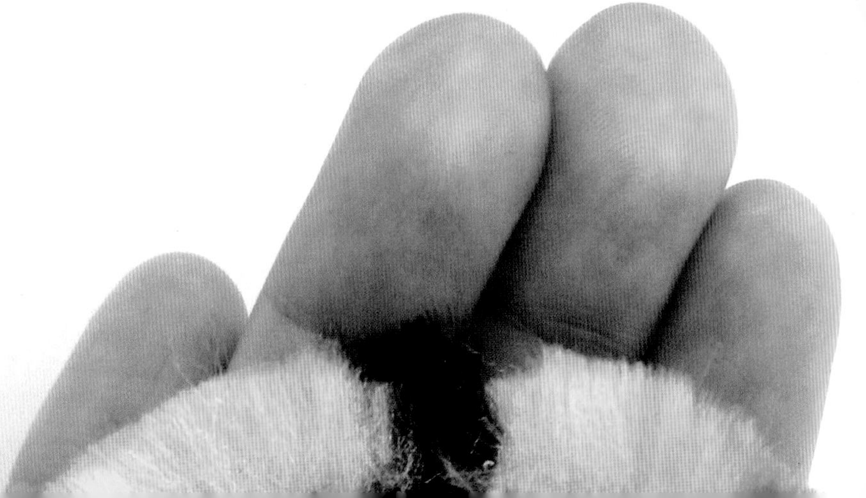

drapery

cloth, pattern,
bedclothes, shawls

Ximena Escobar (COL) escobar.ximena@gmail.com

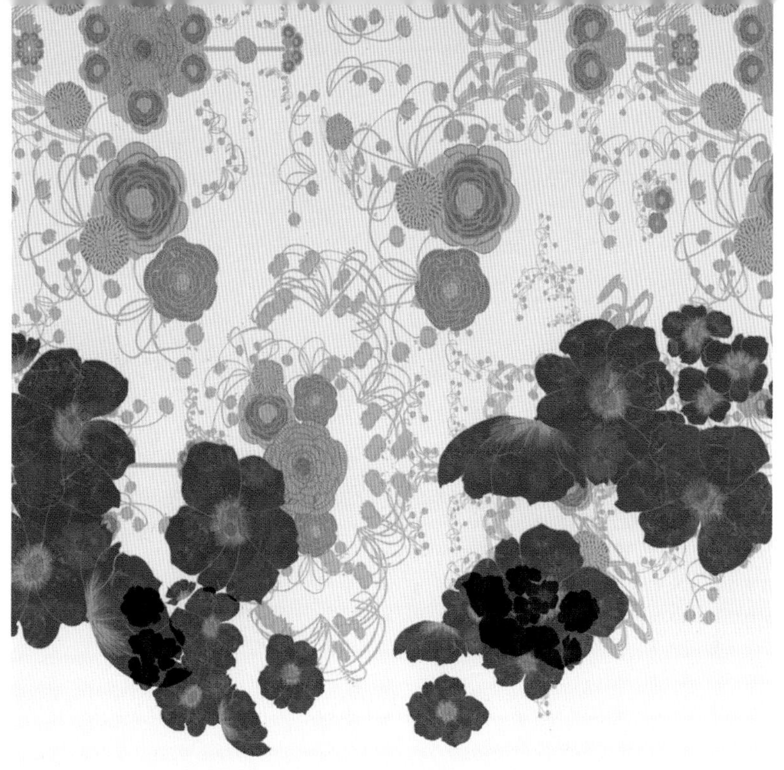

Ximena Escobar (COL) escobar.ximena@gmail.com

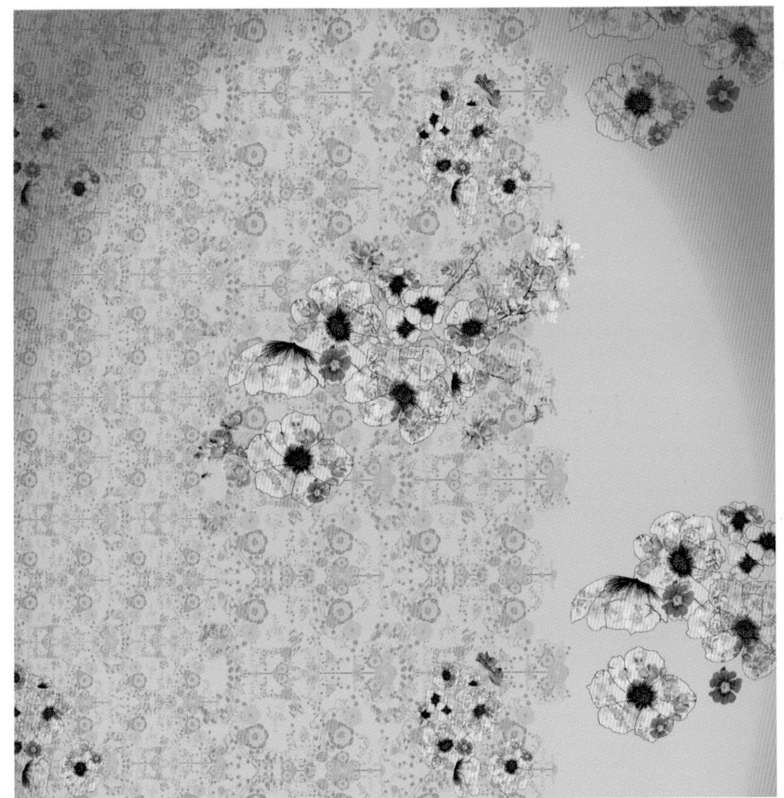

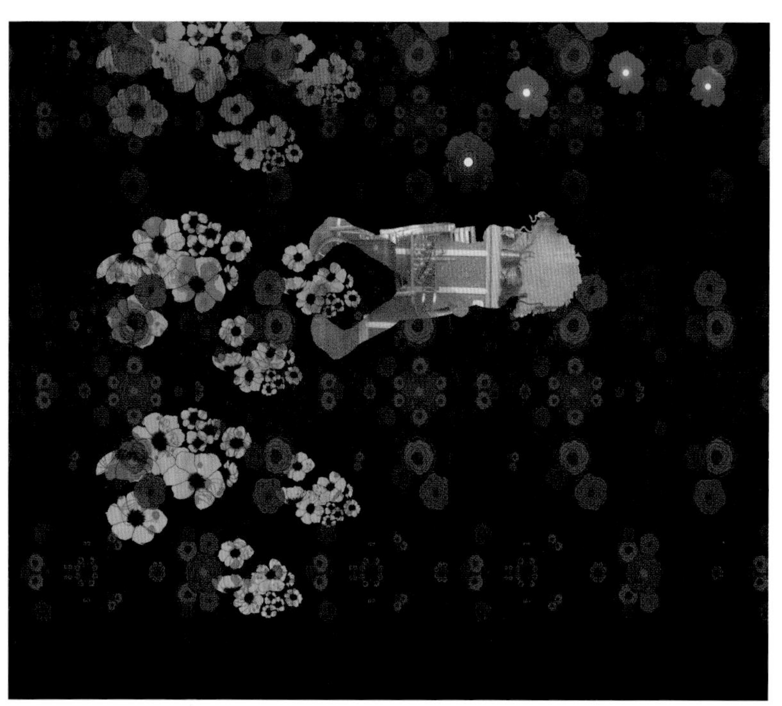

Ximena Escobar (COL) escobar.ximena@gmail.com

Olivier Arcioli (GER) www.o-j-s.com

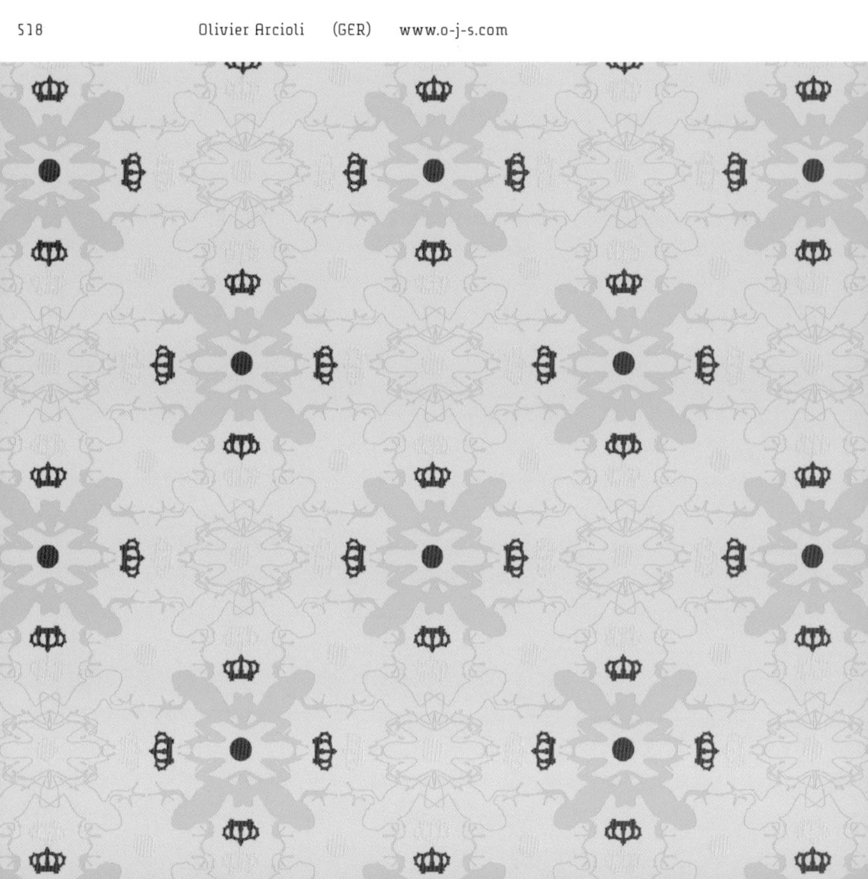

Jessie Churchill (GBR) www.flickr.com/photos/jessiechurchill

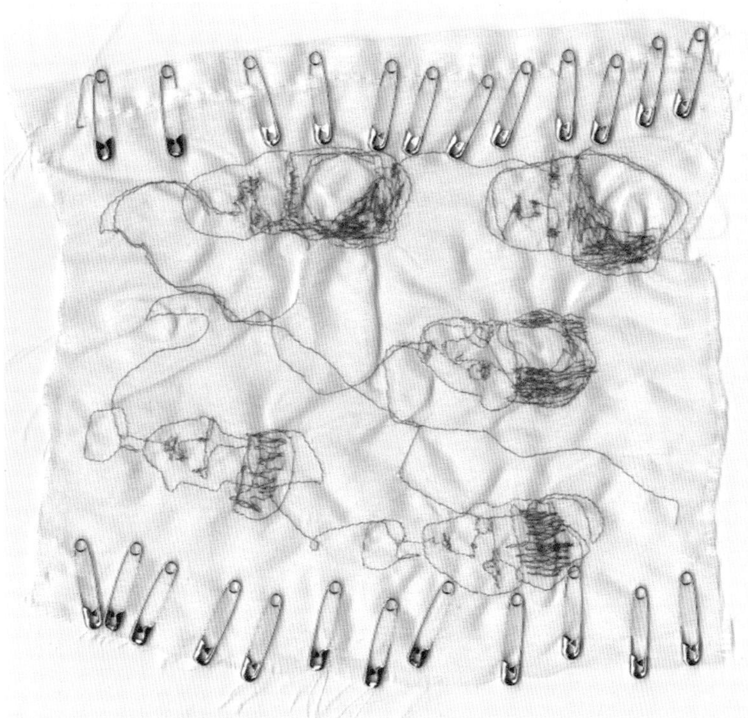

Jessie Churchill (GBR) www.flickr.com/photos/jessiechurchill

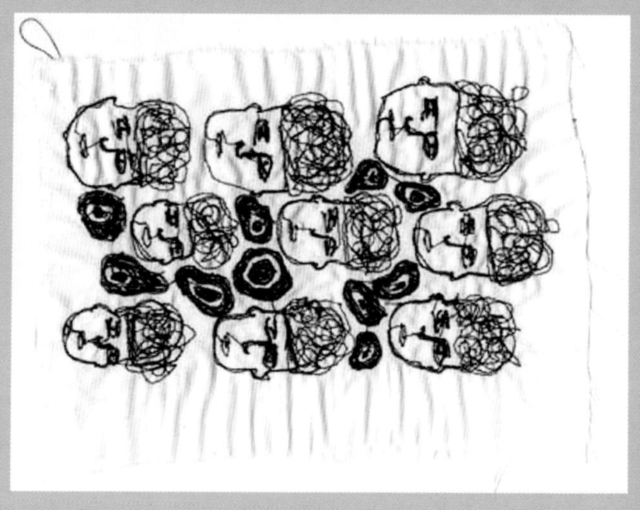

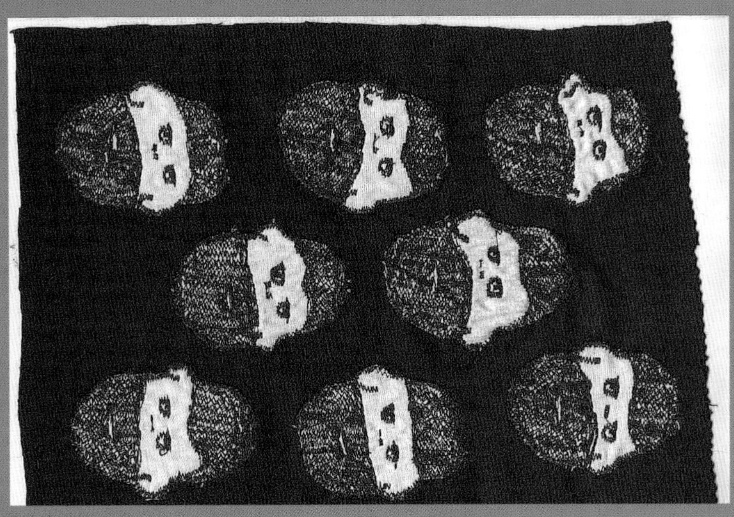

Itxaso Torrontegui Palacios (GER) www.itxasotorrontegui.blogspot.com

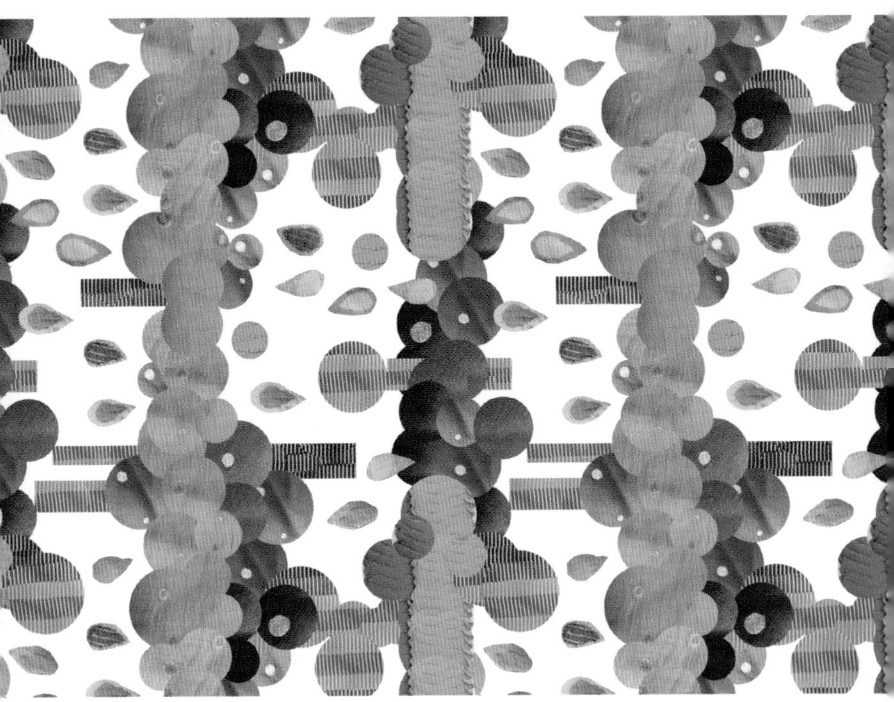

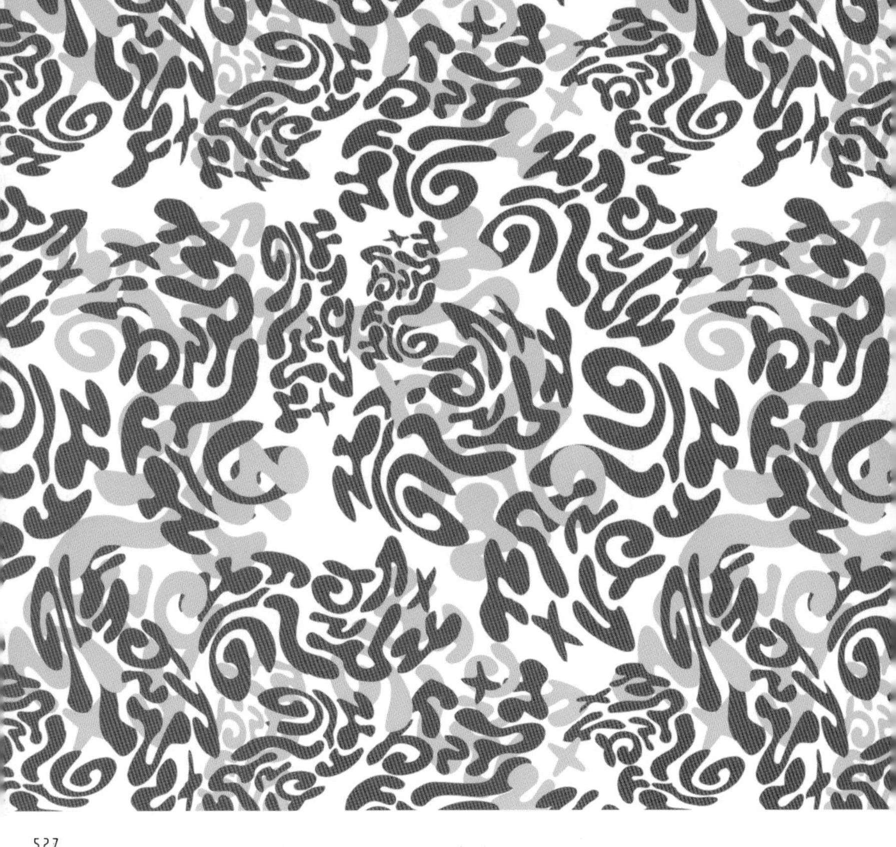

Friends in the narrow space

 Anukun Hamala (THA) www.nokhookdesign.com

Jelly
@cm
www.thejell
ellyproject.com
GSTERS

Anukun Hamala (THA) www.nokhookdesign.com

Josephine Kimberling (USA) www.josephinekimberling.com

535 Natalie Horsman (GBR) www.le-petit-oiseau.blogspot.com

Natalie Horsman (GBR) www.le-petit-oiseau.blogspot.com

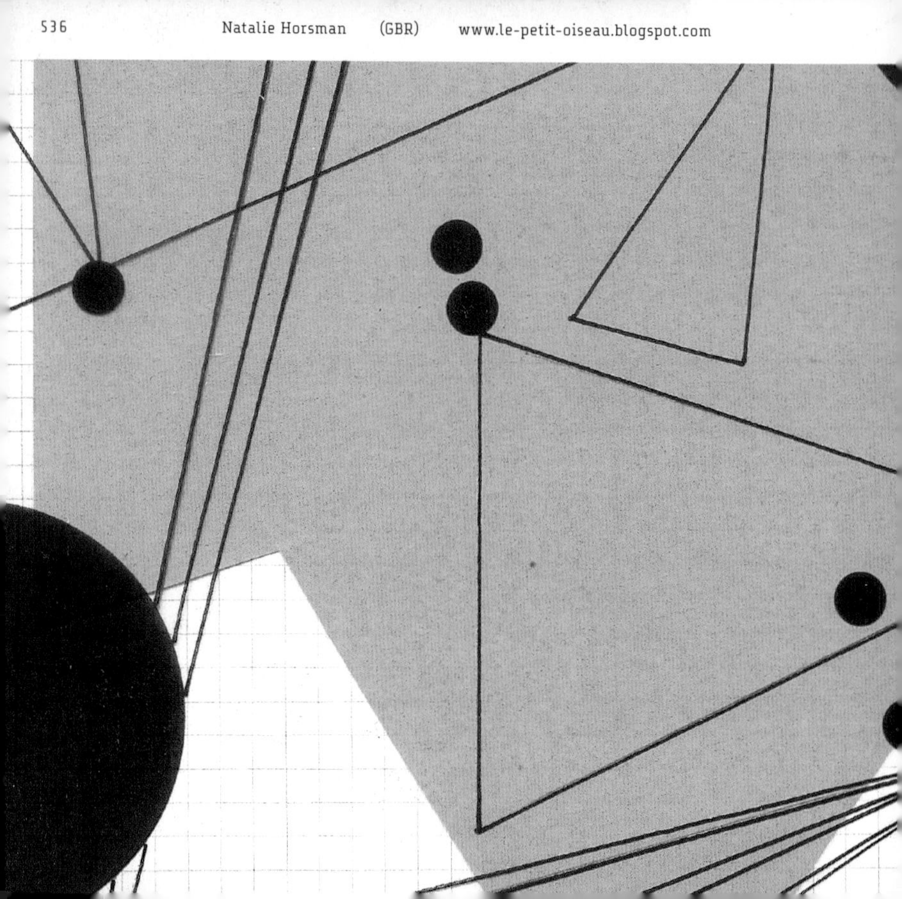

Natalie Horsman (GBR) www.le-petit-oiseau.blogspot.com

Emma Johansson (AUS) www.emmasink.com

Emma Johansson (AUS) www.emmasink.com

Emma Johansson (AUS) www.emmasink.com

545 Eva Pfriem (GER) Evapfriem@web.de

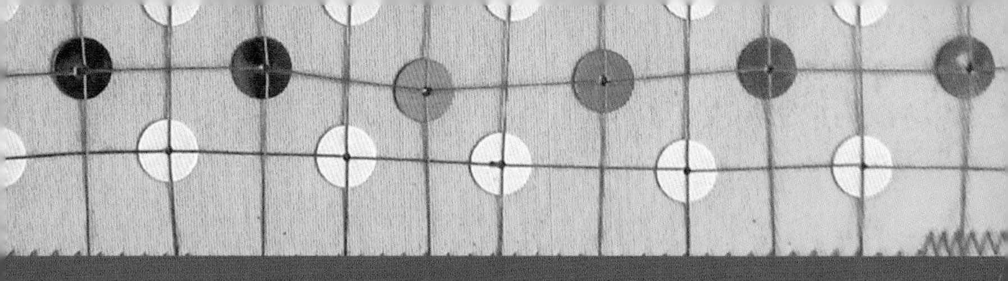

547 Eva Pfriem (GER) Evapfriem@web.de

Eva Pfriem (GER) Evapfriem@web.de

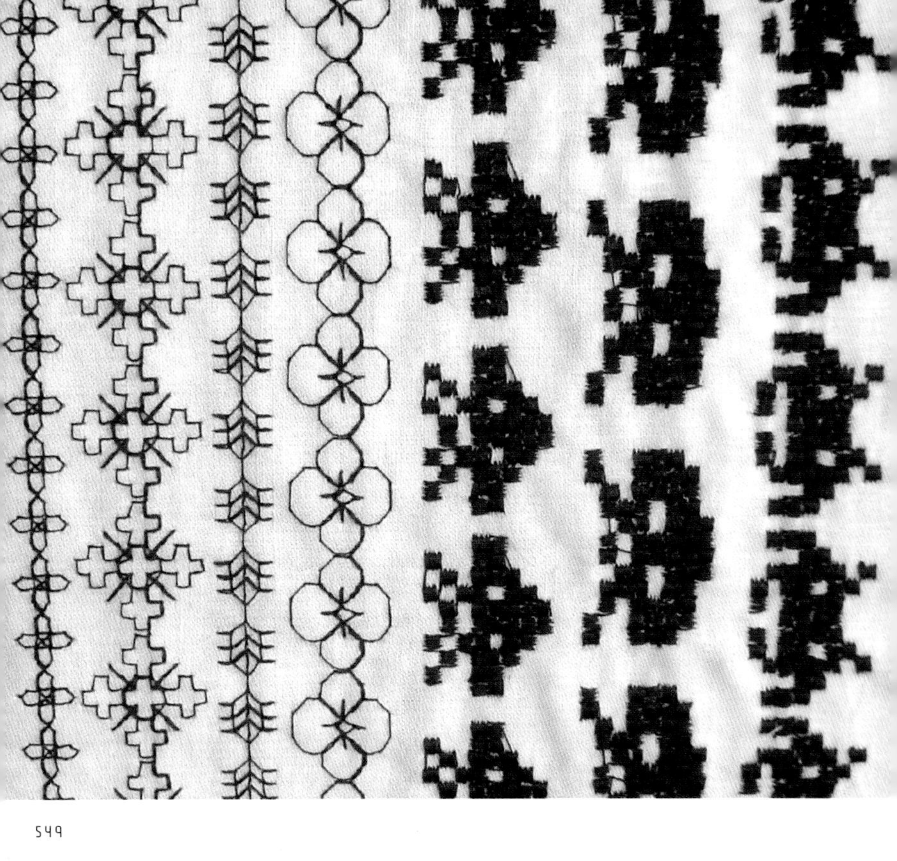

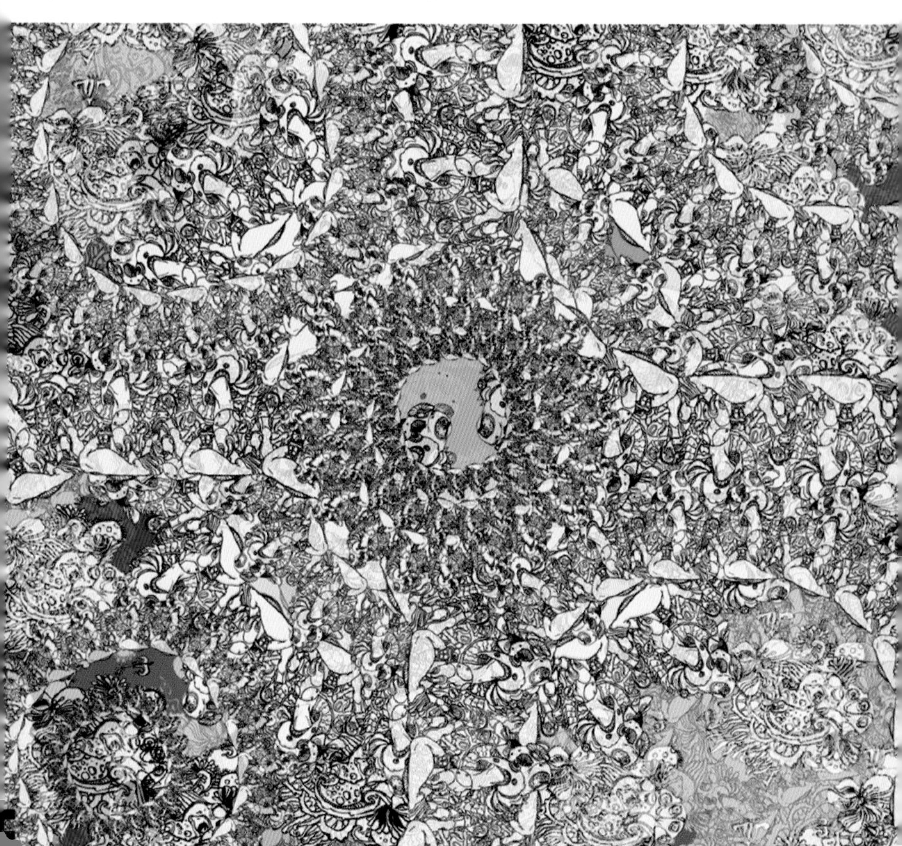

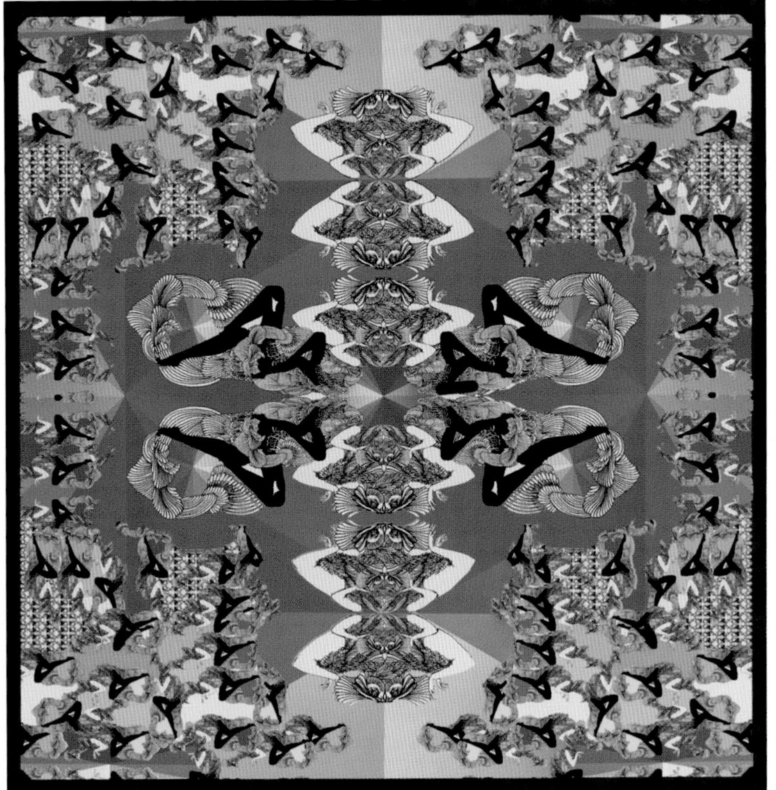

551 Artaksiniya (RUS) www.square-lust.com

Artaksiniya (RUS) www.square-lust.com

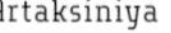

Artaksiniya (RUS) www.square-lust.com

 Zeynep Karaca (GBR) www.figgi.net

DOOM
OH SHIT!
ROCK STEADY

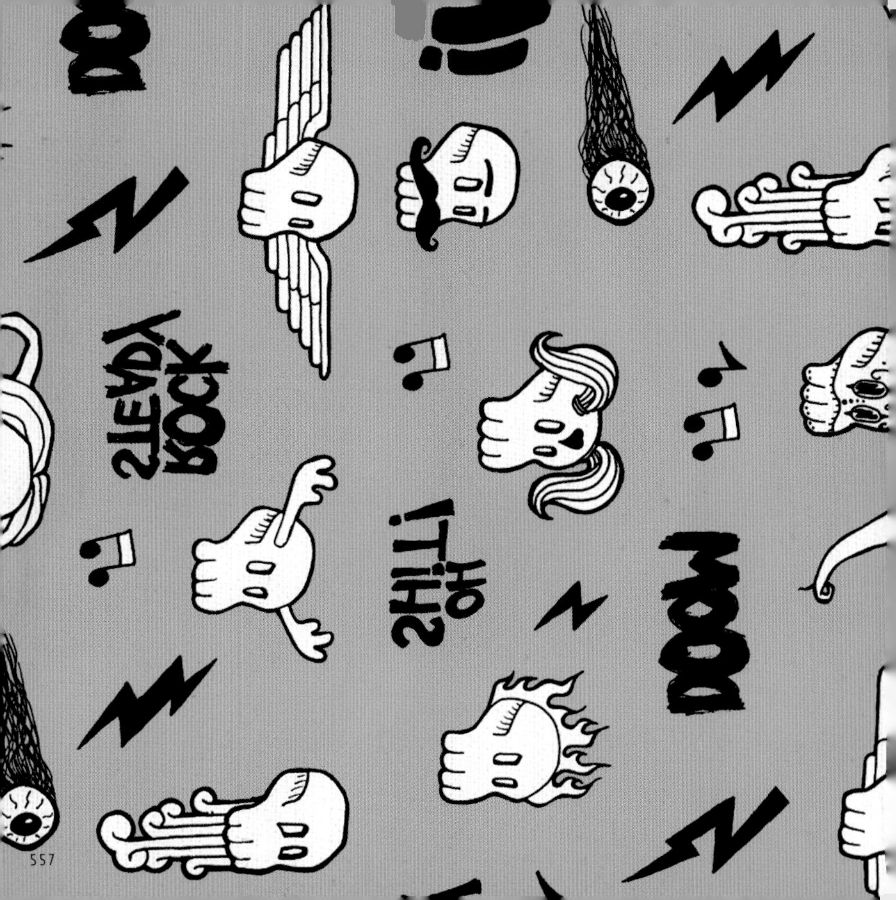
STEADY ROCK
OH SHIT!
DOOM

Erik Bertell (FIN) www.kaamosgroup.fi

Finna Leibenguth (GER) www.wg-atelier.de

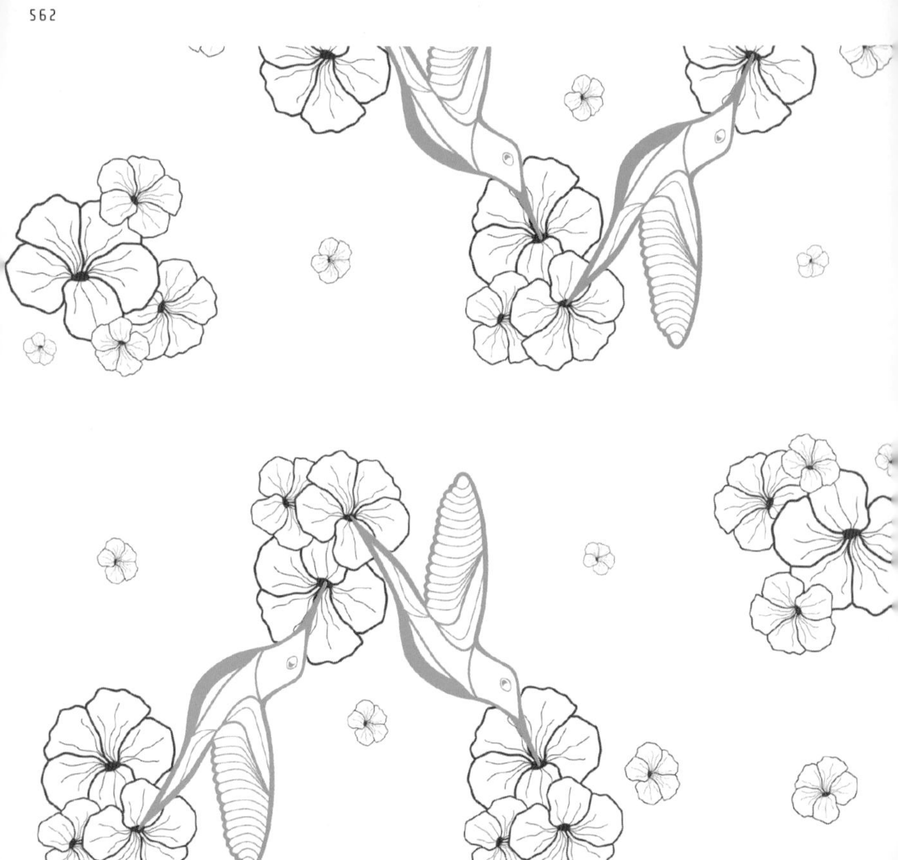

Finna Leibenguth (GER) www.wg-atelier.de

Kätlin Kaljuvee (EE) katlinkaljuvee@gmail.com

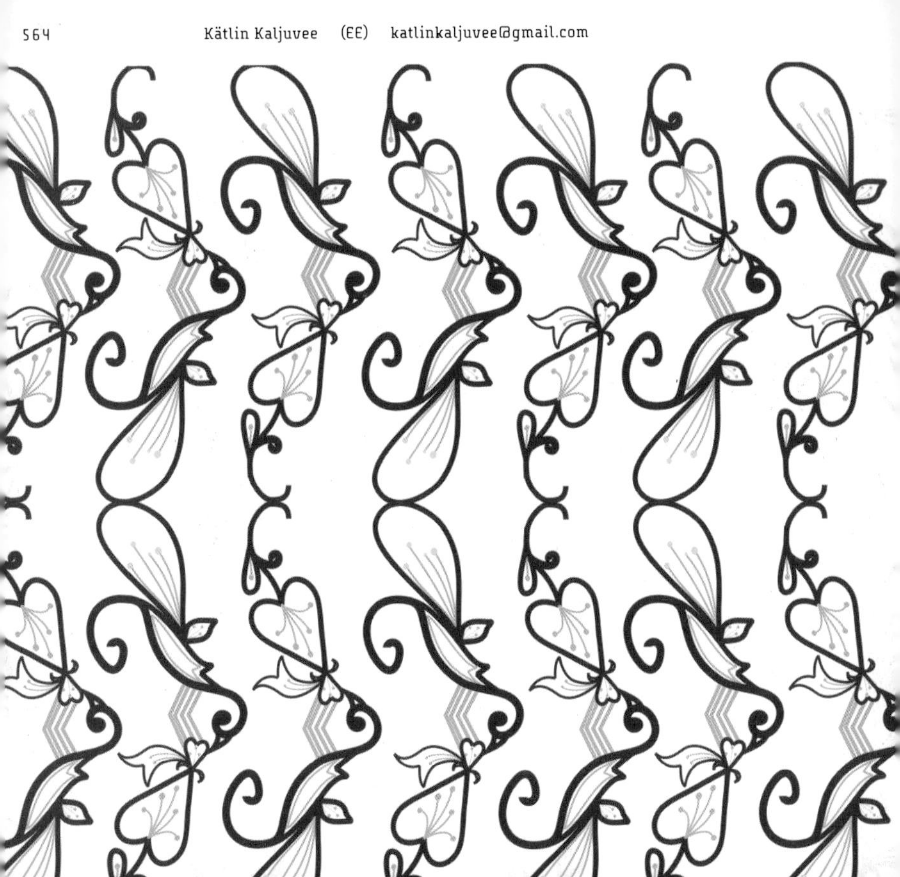

 Kätlin Kaljuvee (EE) katlinkaljuvee@gmail.com

Sylvia Stølan (NED) www.sylviastolan.com

Sylvia Stølan (NED) www.sylviastolan.com

Caroline Täschner (GER) caroline.taeschner@gmx.de

Caroline Täschner (GER) caroline.taeschner@gmx.de

Caroline Täschner (GER) caroline.taeschner@gmx.de

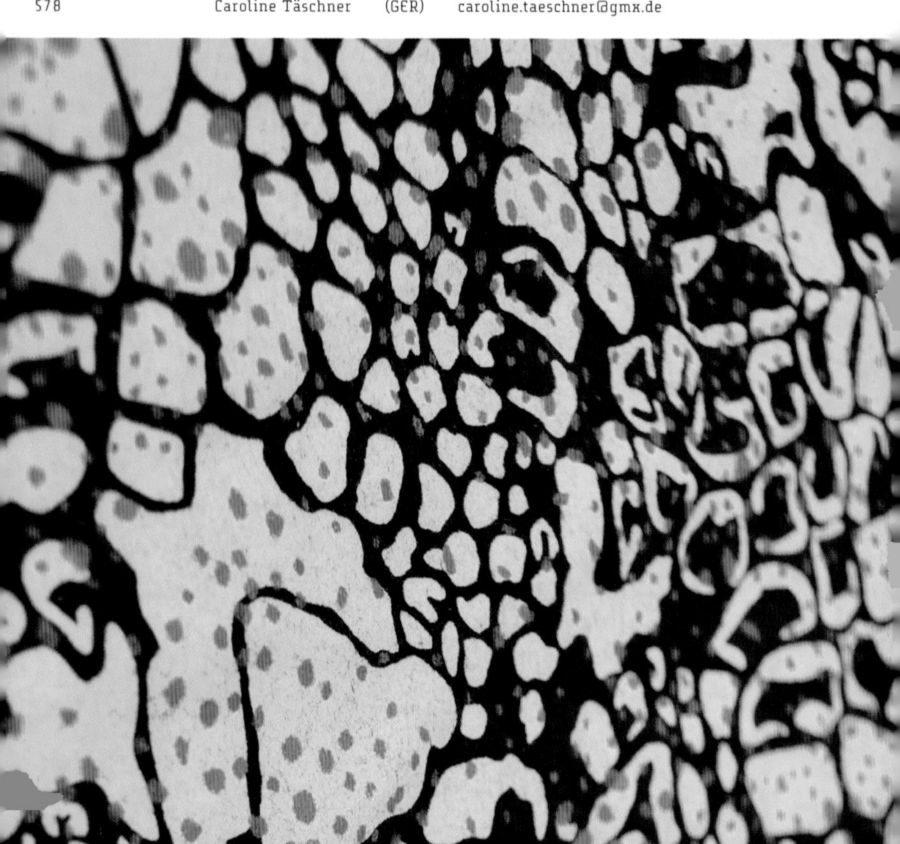

Caroline Täschner (GER) caroline.taeschner@gmx.de

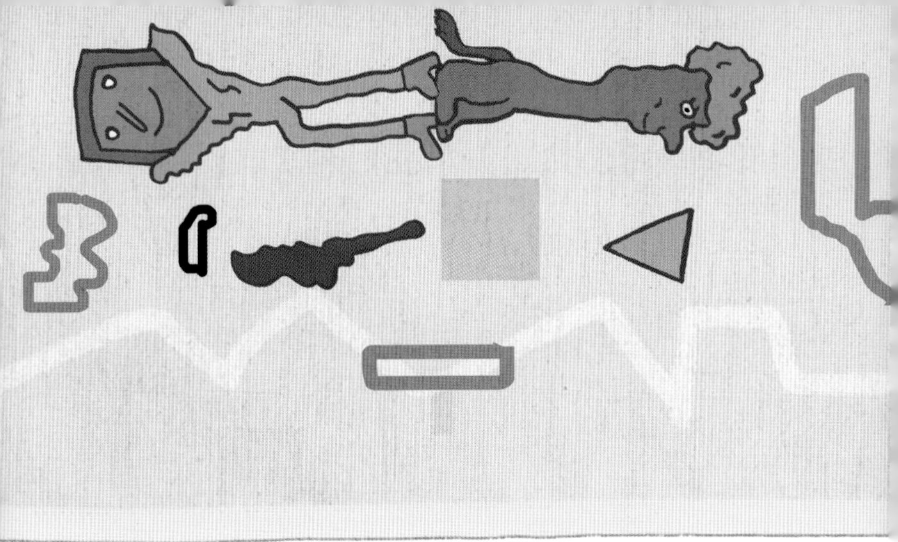

Marie Blanchard (FRA) www.marieblanchard.com

587 Sarah Wade (GBR) www.designhousestudios.co.uk

Sarah Wade (GBR) www.designhousestudios.co.uk

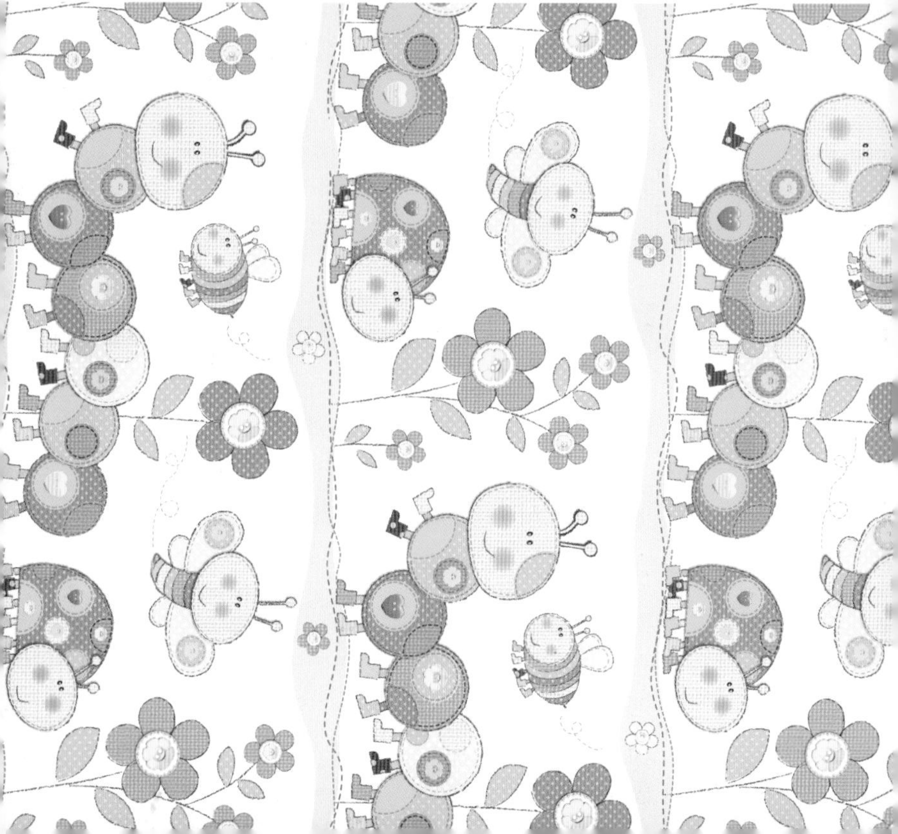

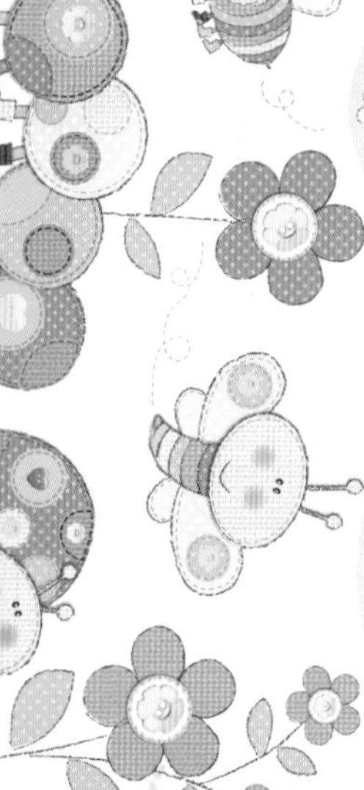

Moo
Oink
Cluck
Eeyore

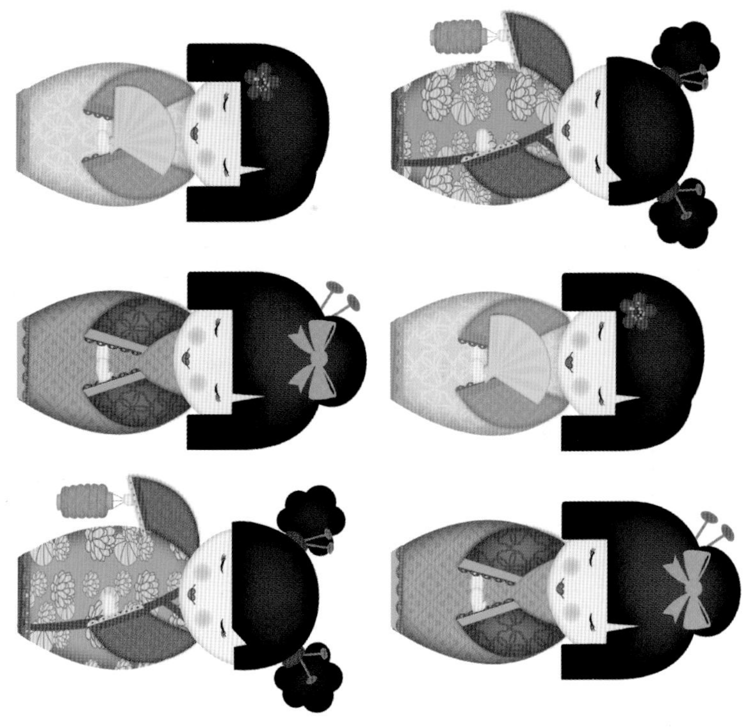

 Sarah Wade (GBR) www.designhousestudios.co.uk

Olivier Arcioli (GER) www.o-j-s.com

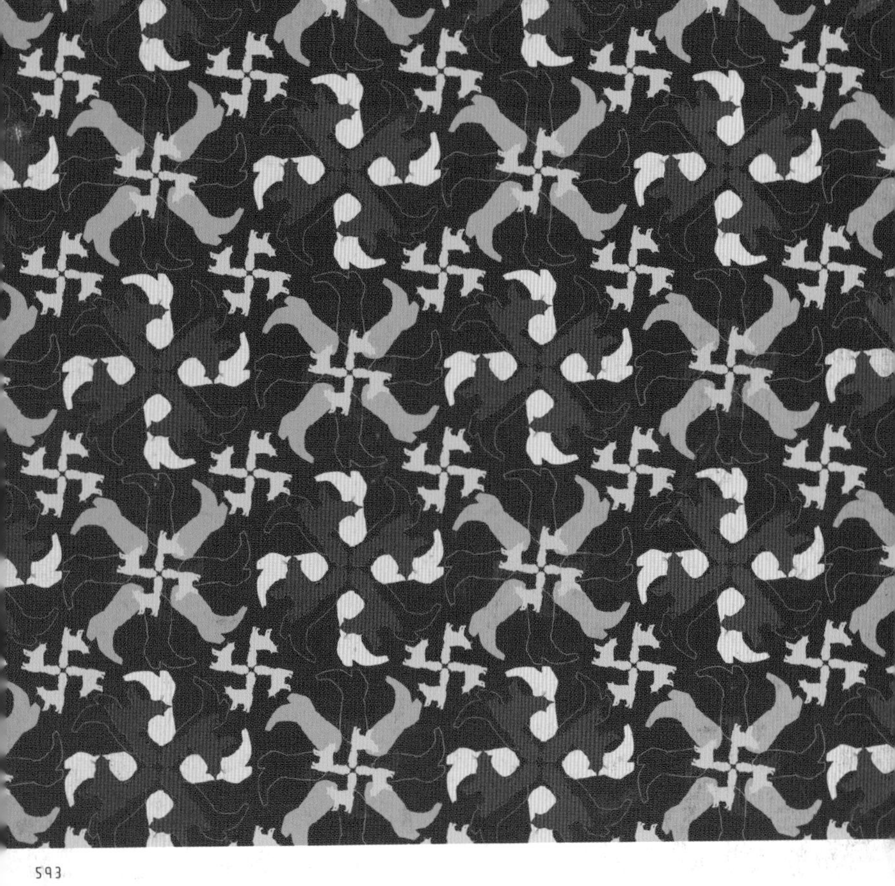

Myriam Lucas (GER) www.myaluc.de

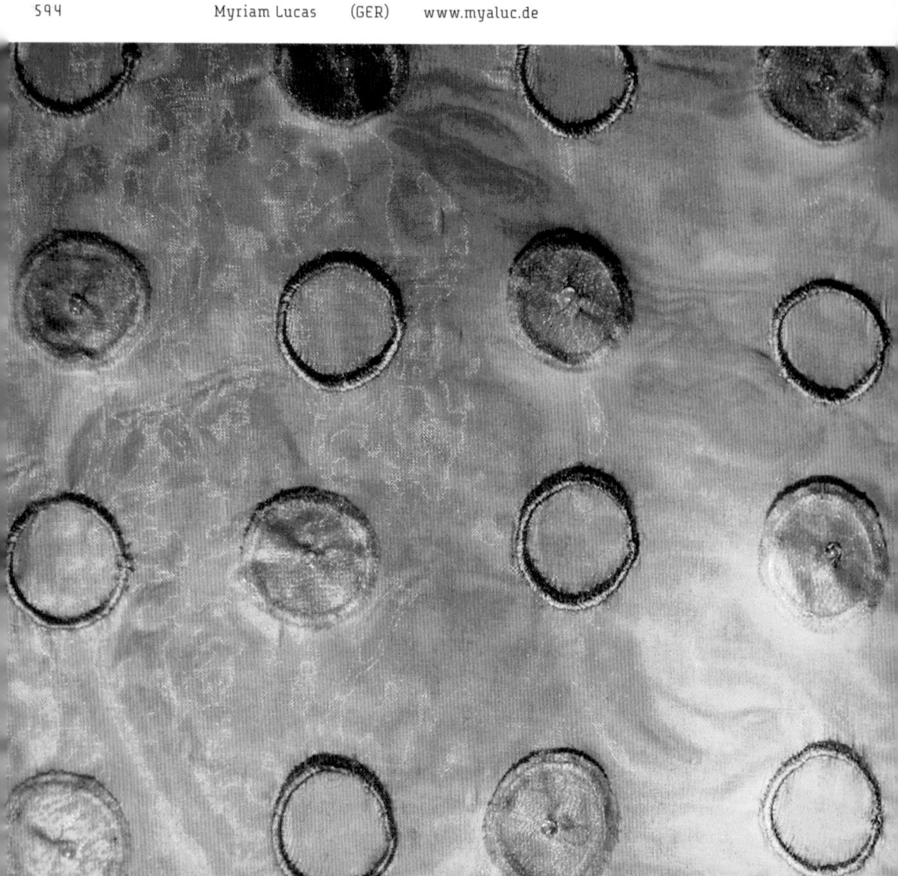

Come in!

597 Ulla Gmeiner (GER) www.telaire.blogspot.com

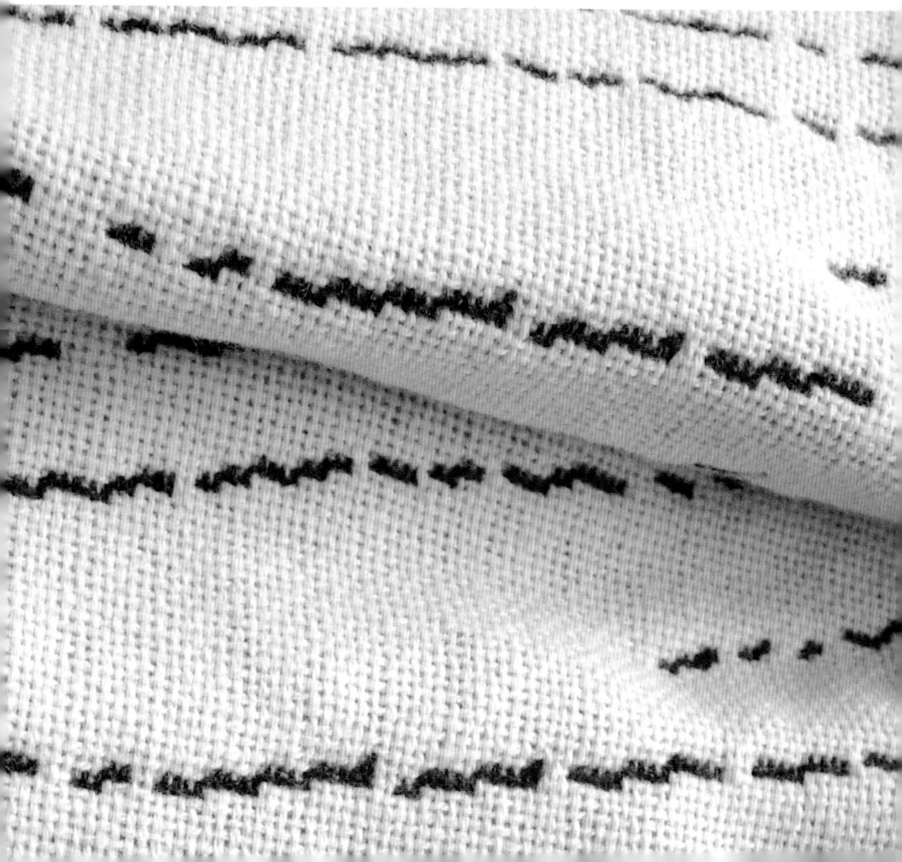

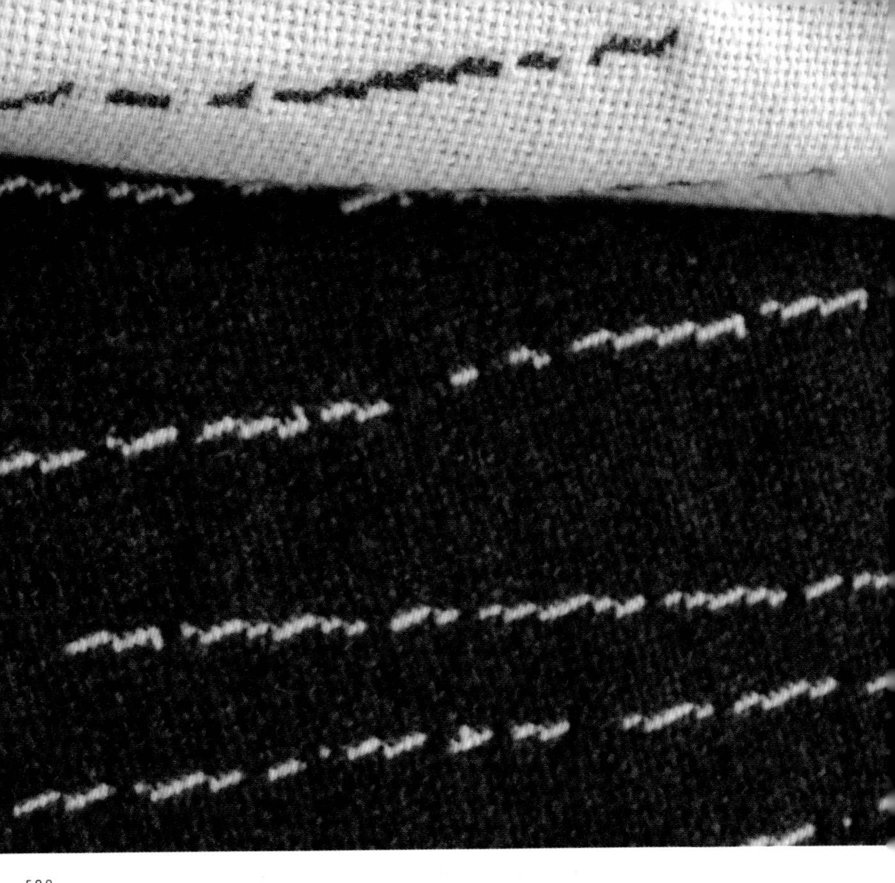

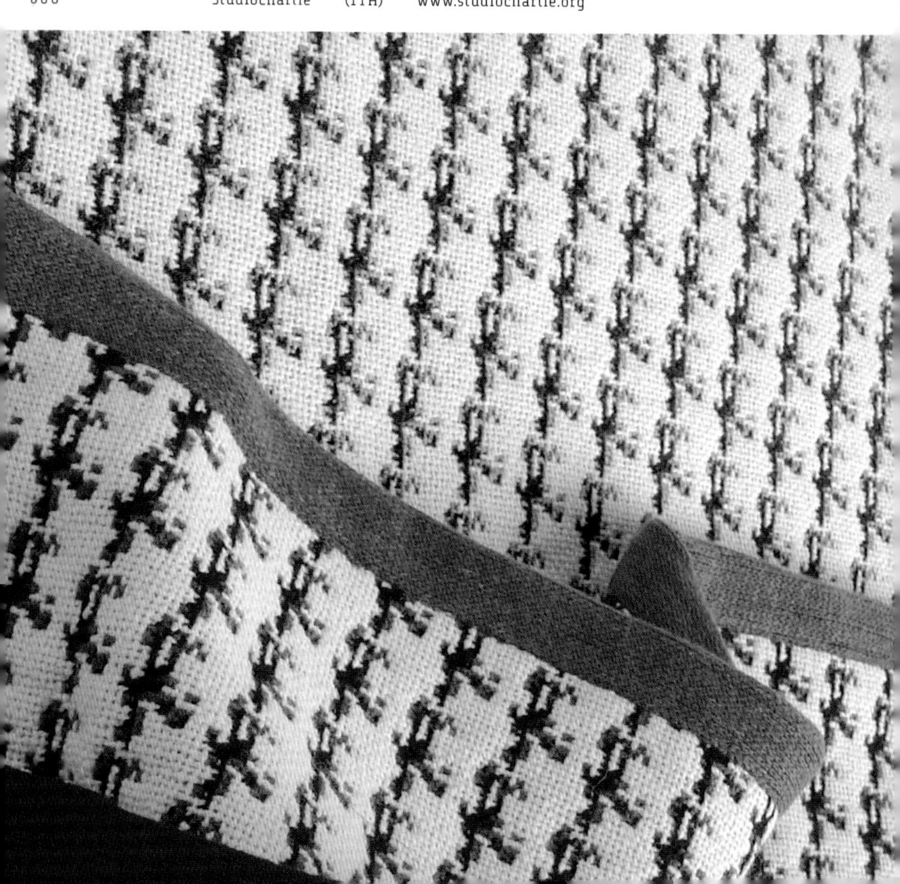

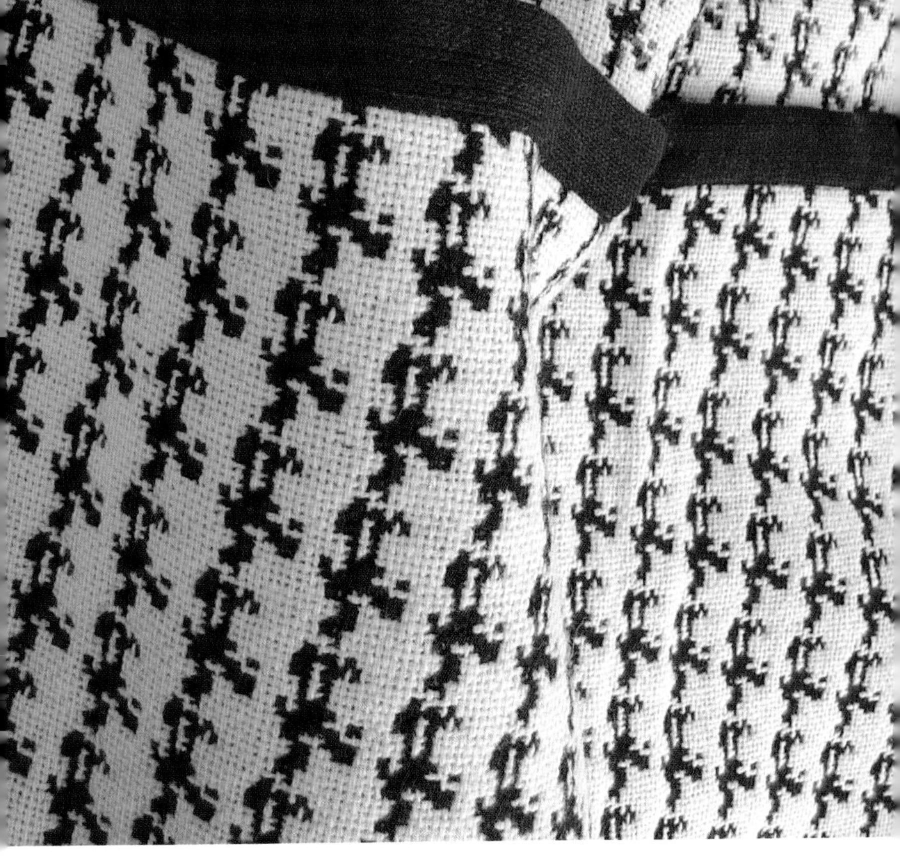

Sarah Wade (GBR) www.designhousestudios.co.uk

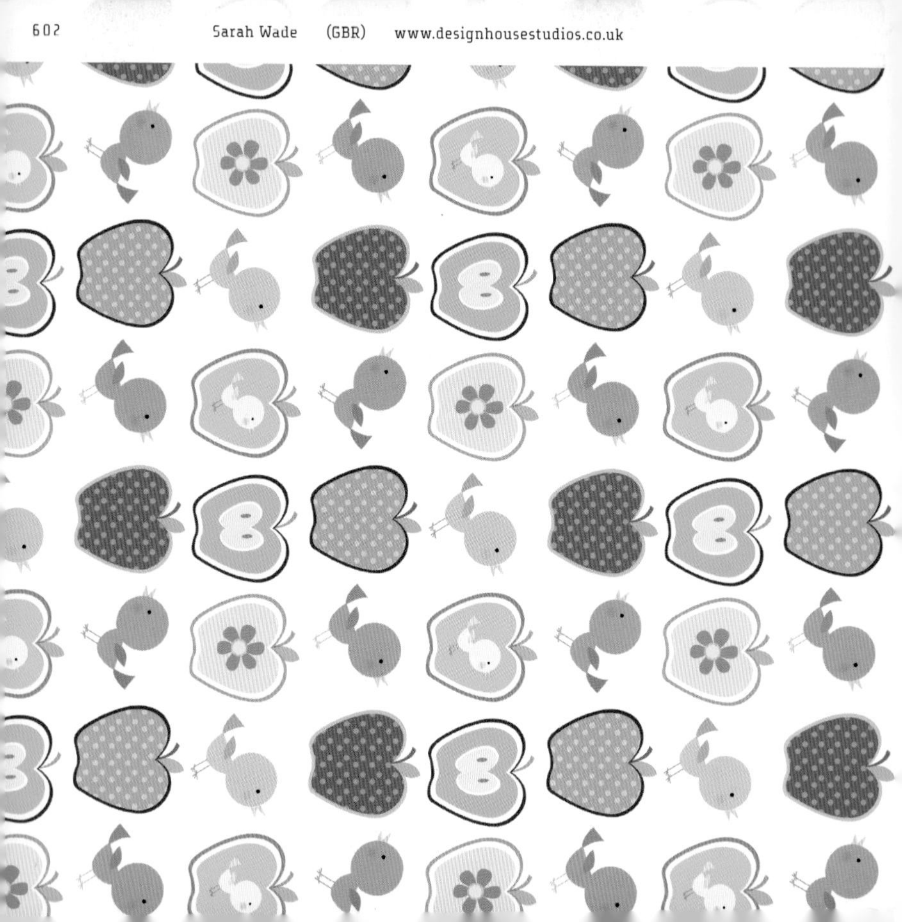

Janine Rewell (FIN) www.janinerewell.com

Sarah Wade (GBR) www.designhousestudios.co.uk

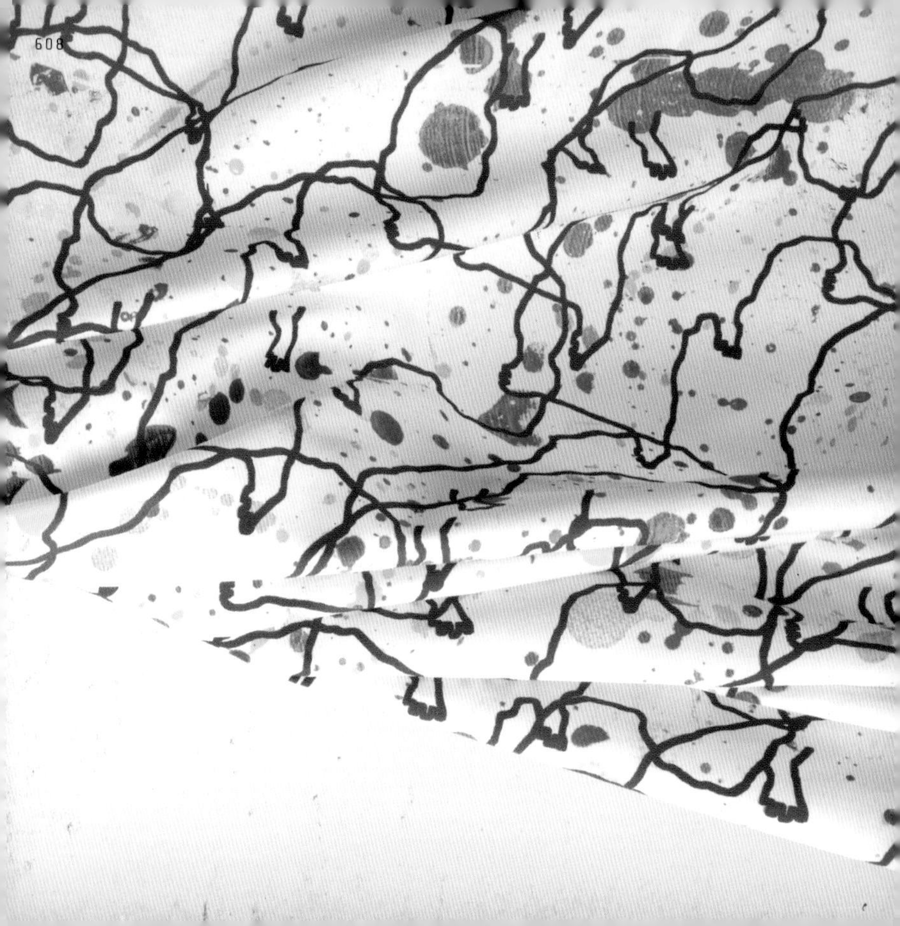

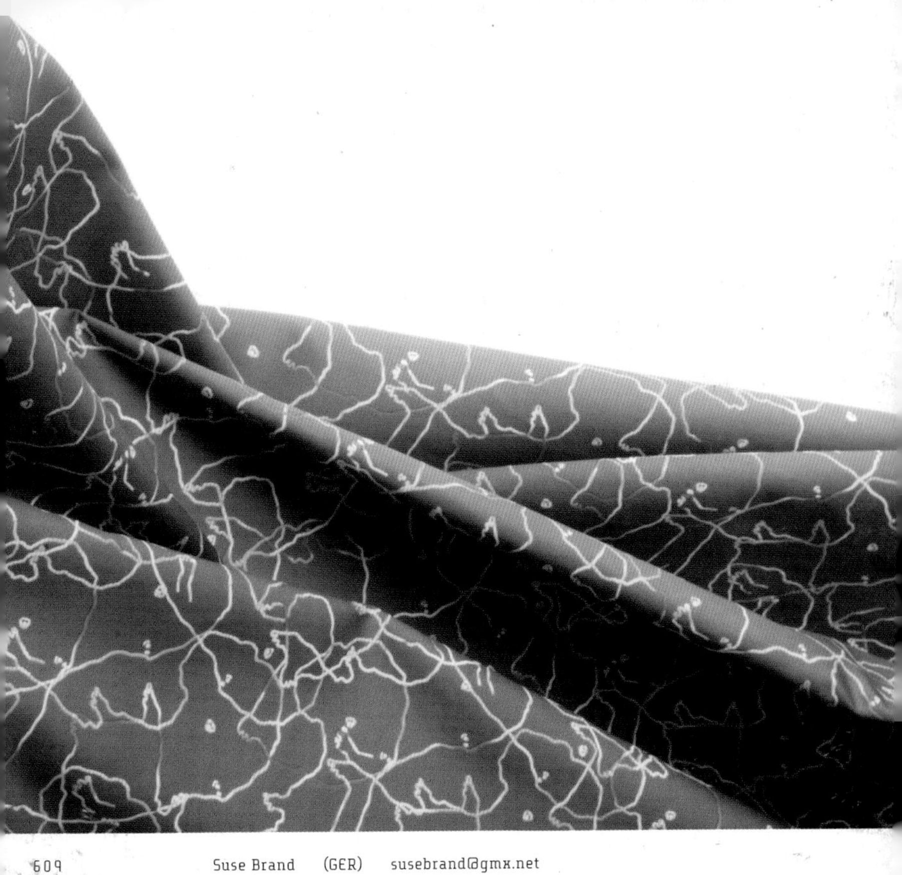

Suse Brand (GER) susebrand@gmx.net

610 Suse Brand (GER) susebrand@gmx.net

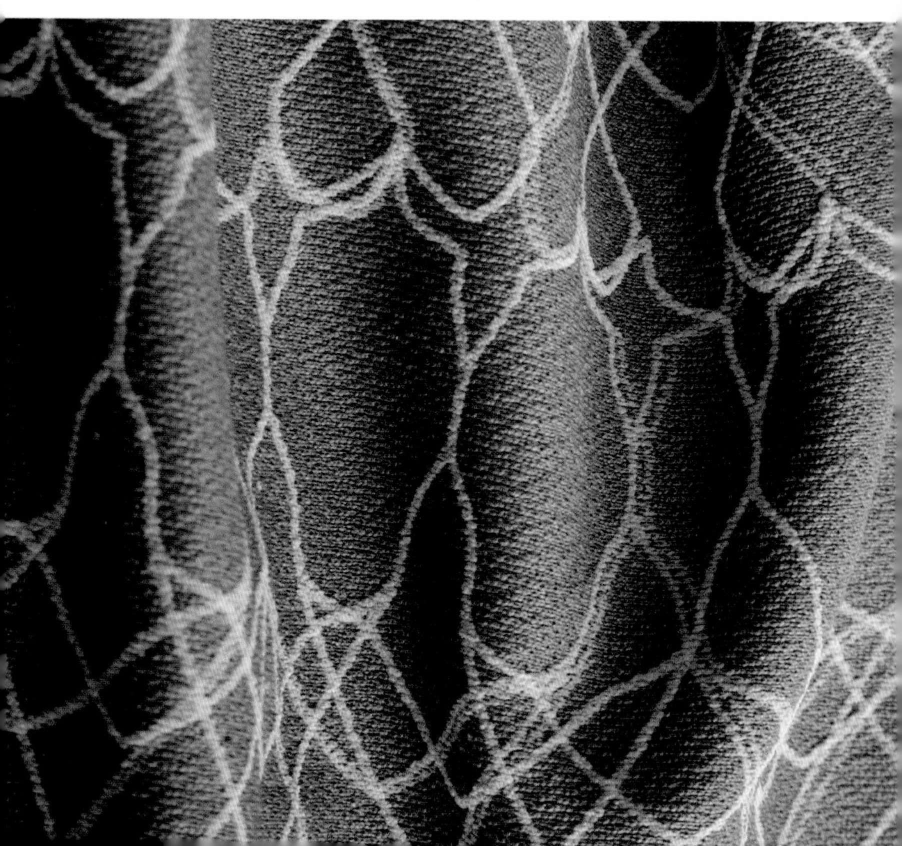

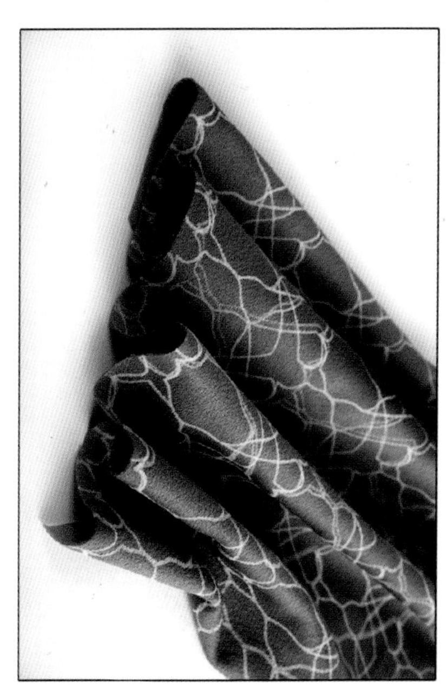

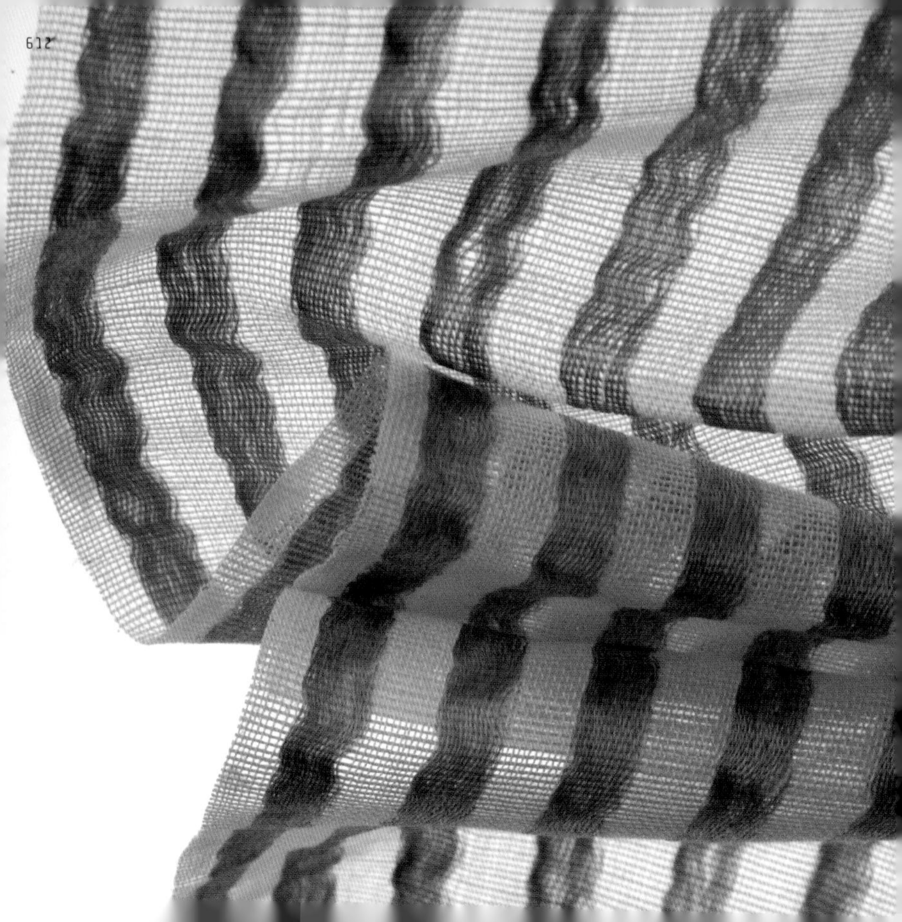

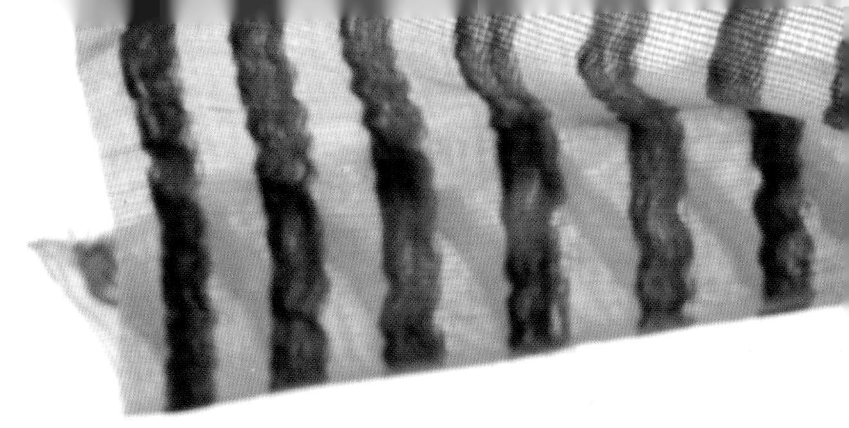

Suse Brand (GER) susebrand@gmx.net

Suse Brand (GER) susebrand@gmx.net

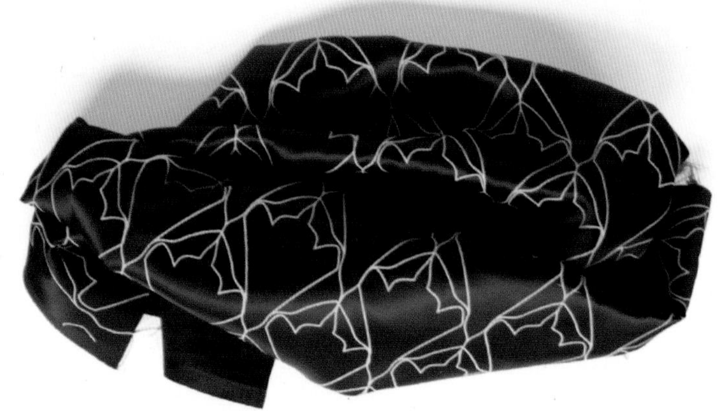

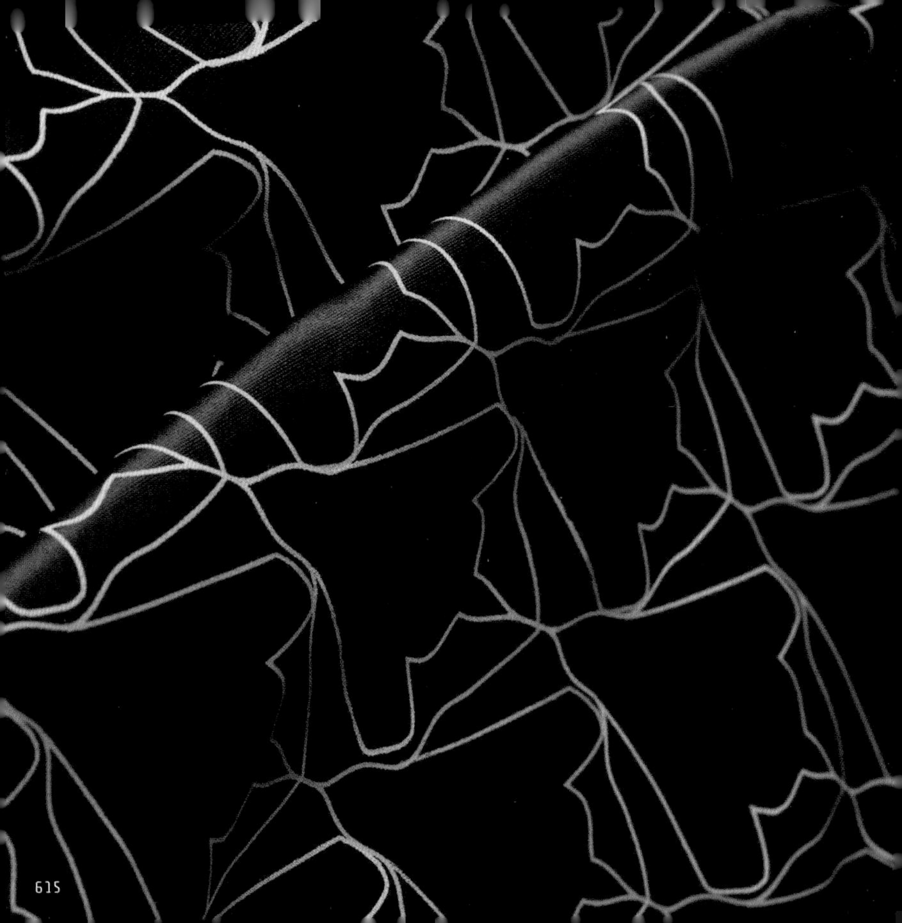

Itxaso Torrontegui Palacios (GER) www.itxasotorrontegui.blogspot.com

Joel Mackenzie (CAN) www.ijoelamackenzie@gmail.com

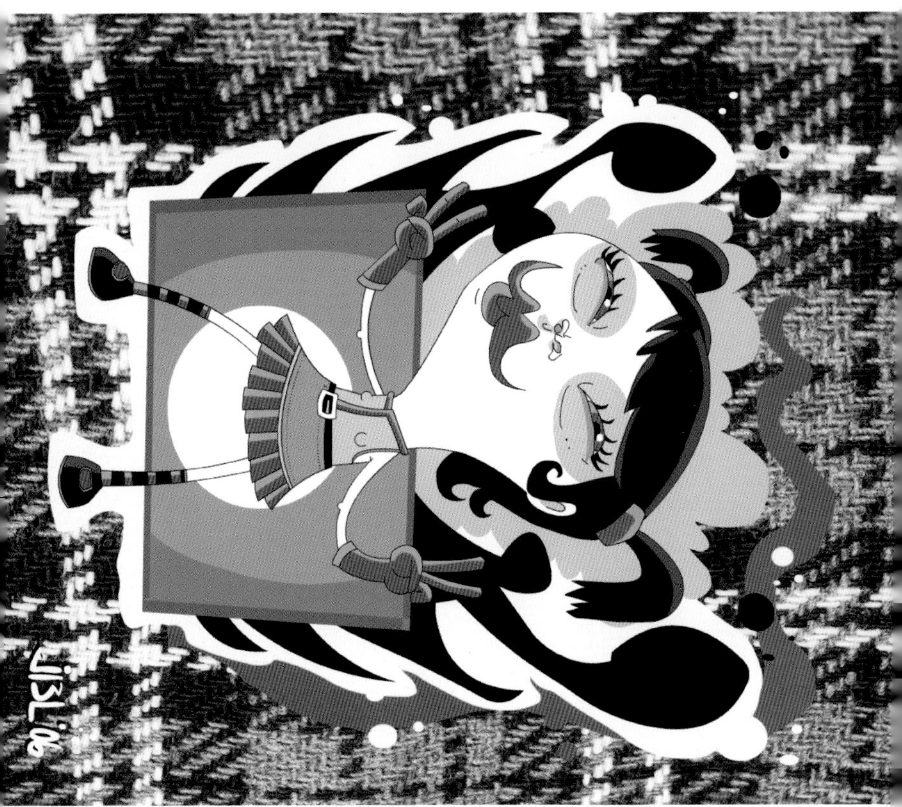

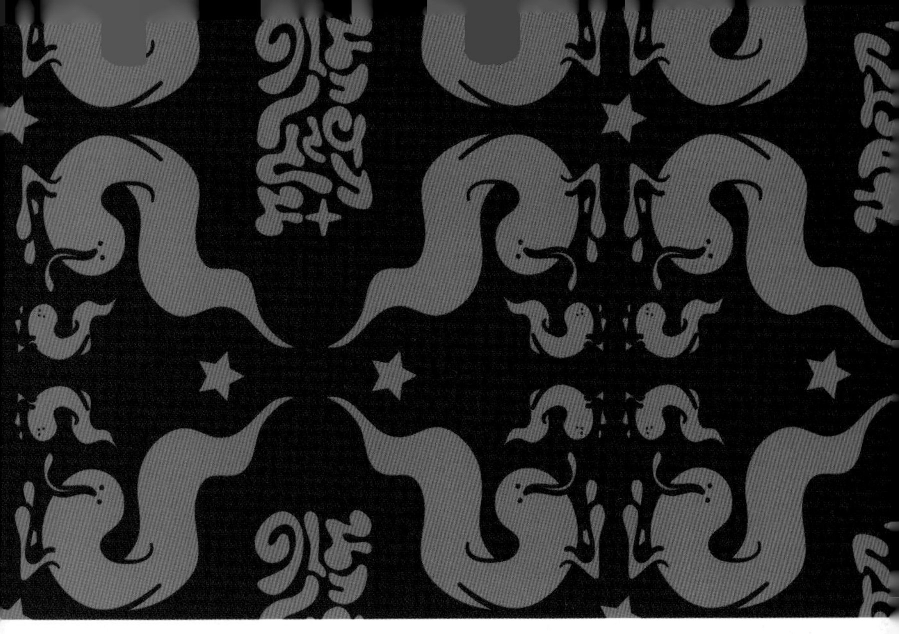

Anukun Hamala (THA) www.nokhookdesign.com

Anukun Hamala (THA) www.nokhookdesign.com

Rossella Sferlazzo (ITA) www.sferlazzorossella.wordpress.com/

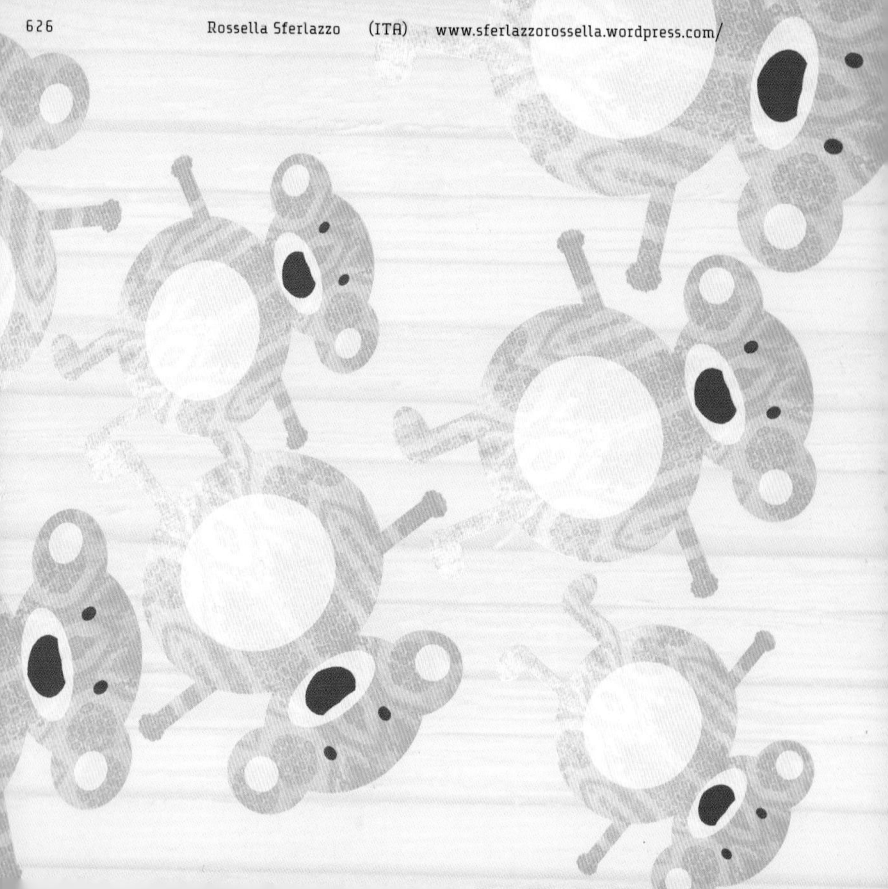

Christian Frank Müller (GER) cfmrex@web.de

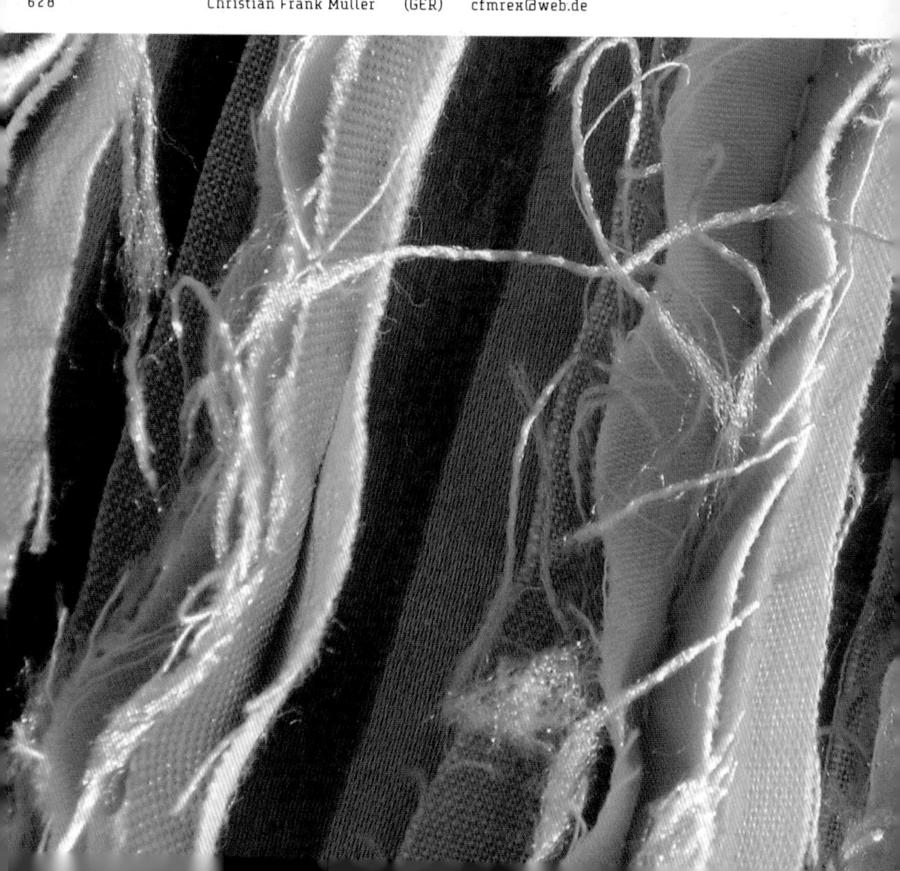

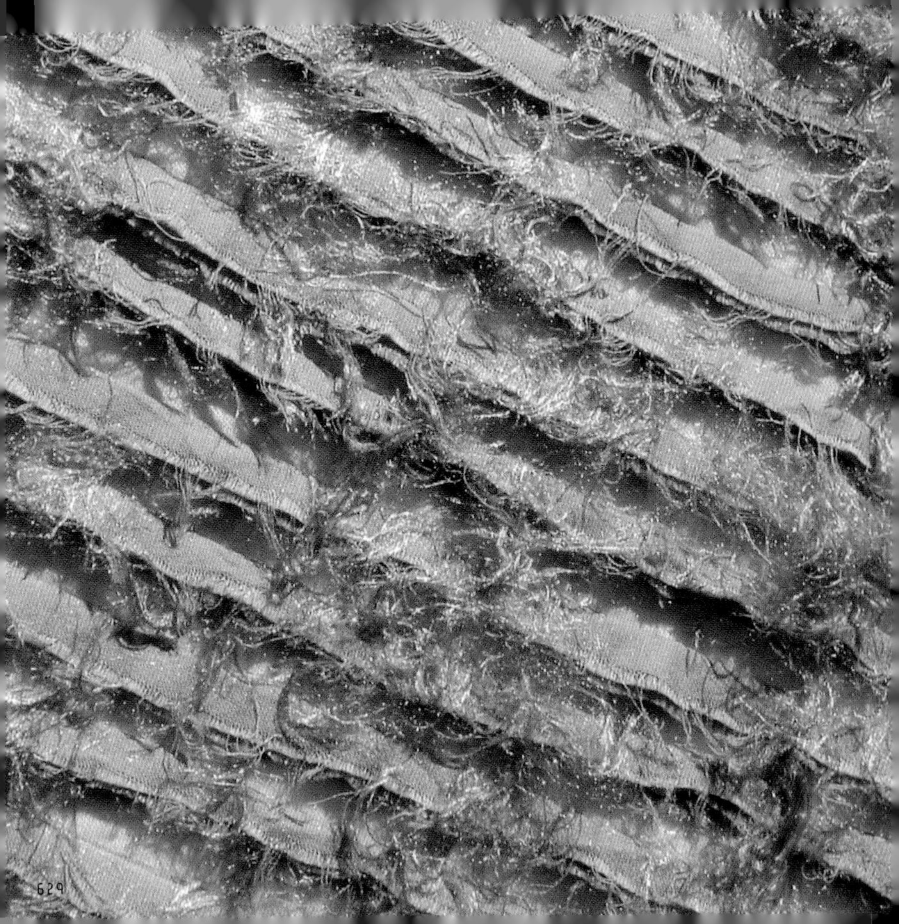

631 Christian Frank Müller (GER) cfmrex@web.de

Christian Frank Müller (GER) cfmrex@web.de

Katja Kurochkina (GER) www.kurochkina.com

Katja Kurochkina (GER) www.kurochkina.com

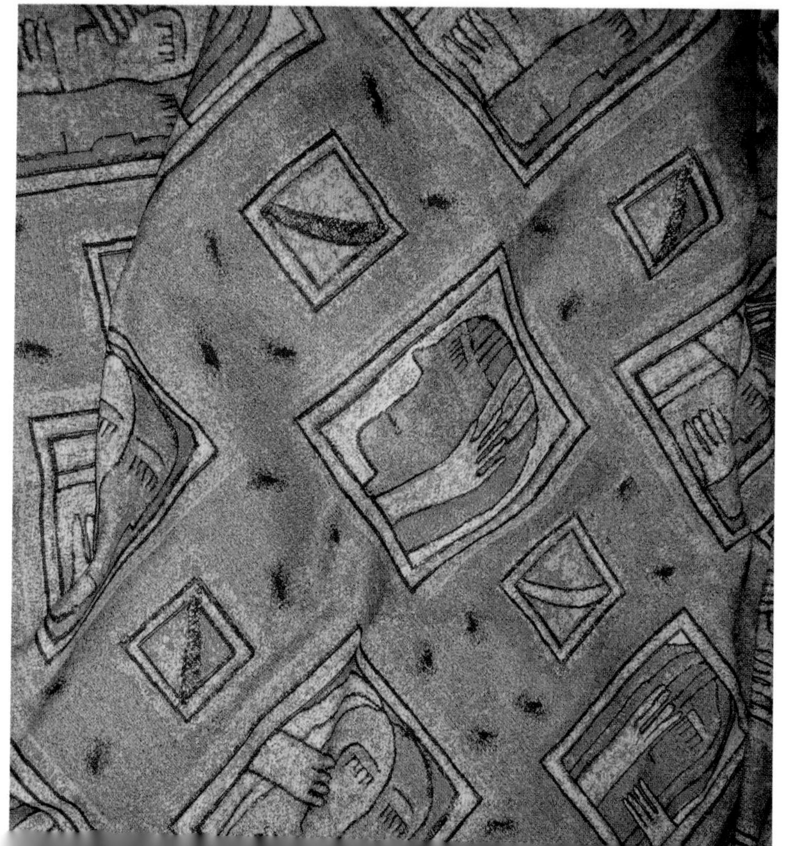

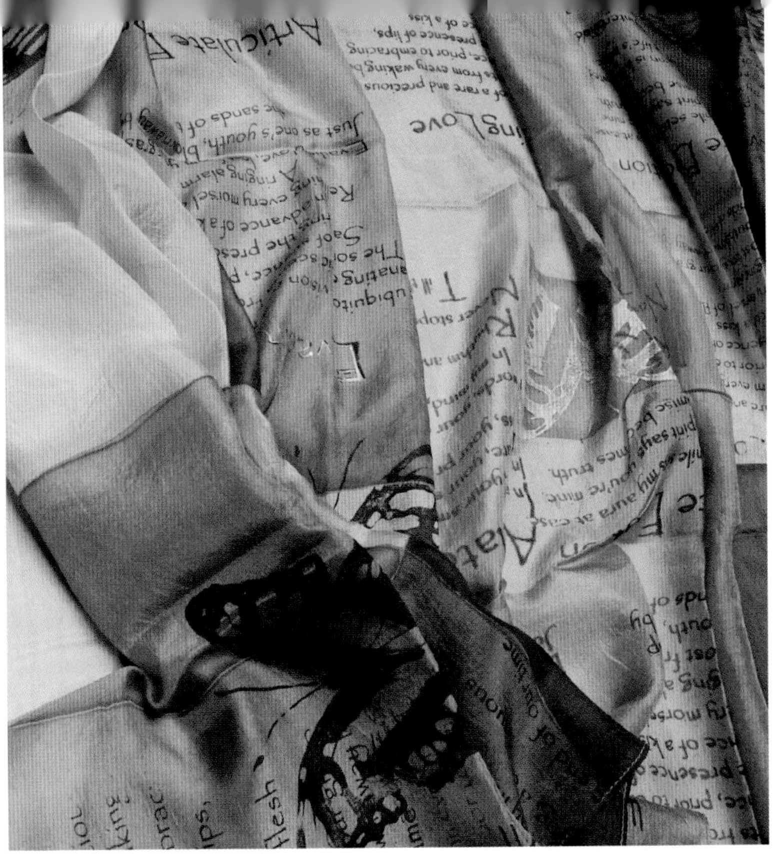

639 Uta Tischendorf (GER) utatischendorf@gmx.de

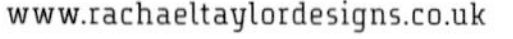

Rachael Taylor (GBR) www.rachaeltaylordesigns.co.uk

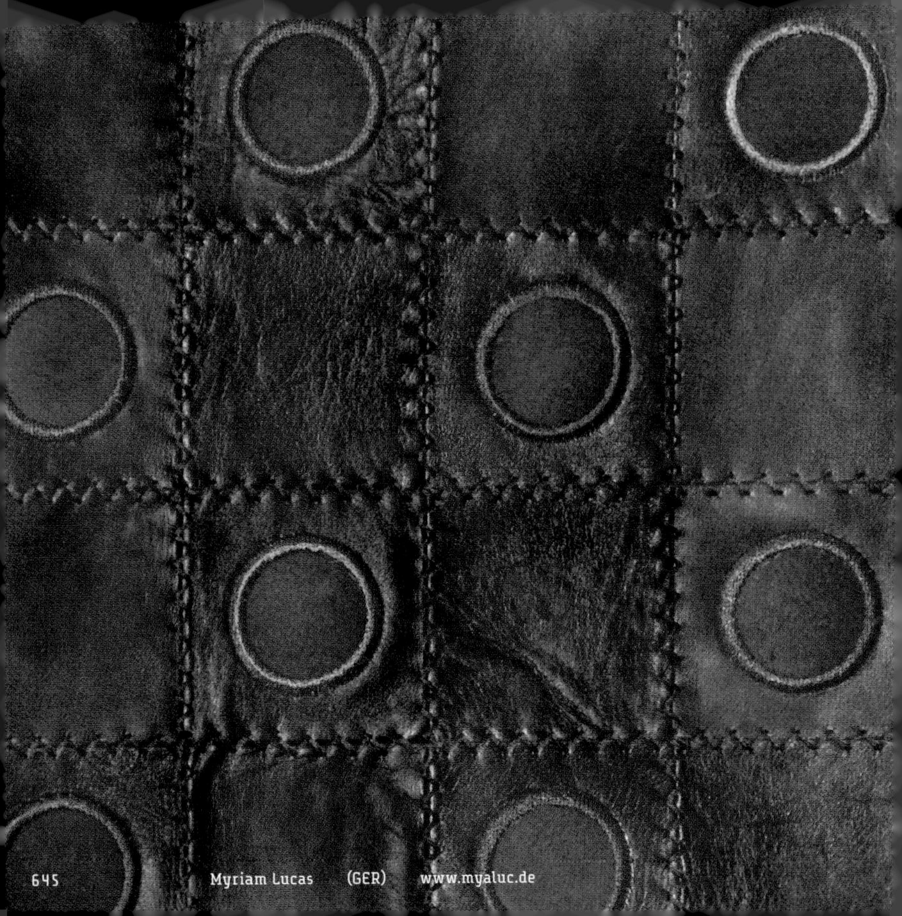

Myriam Lucas (GER) www.myaluc.de

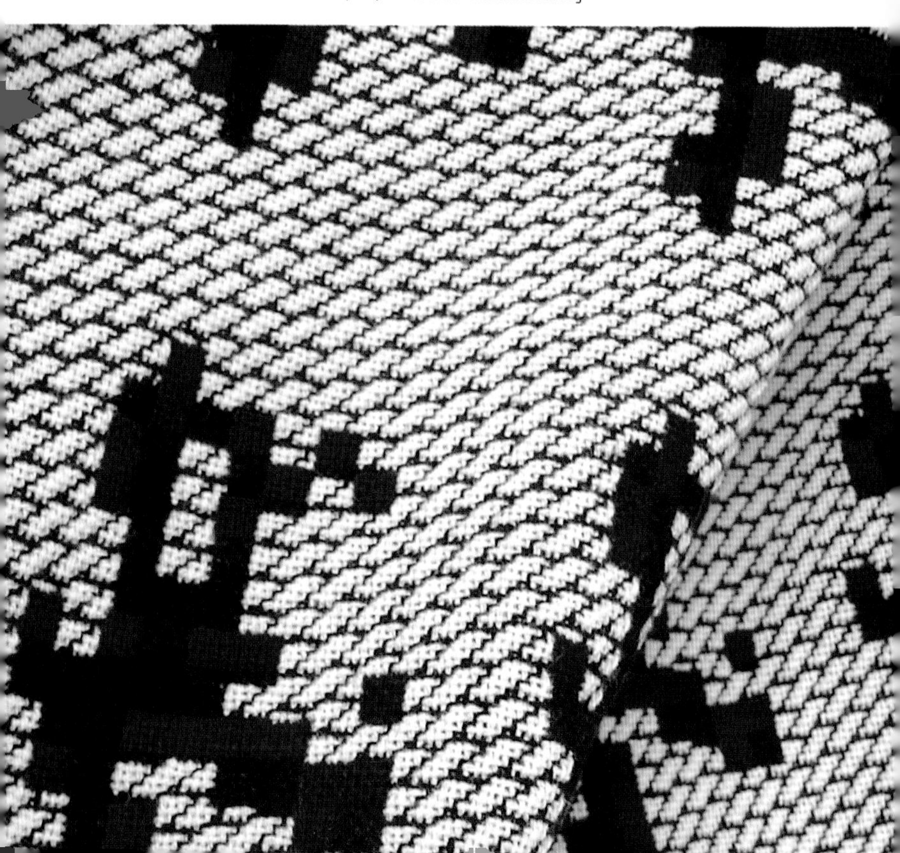

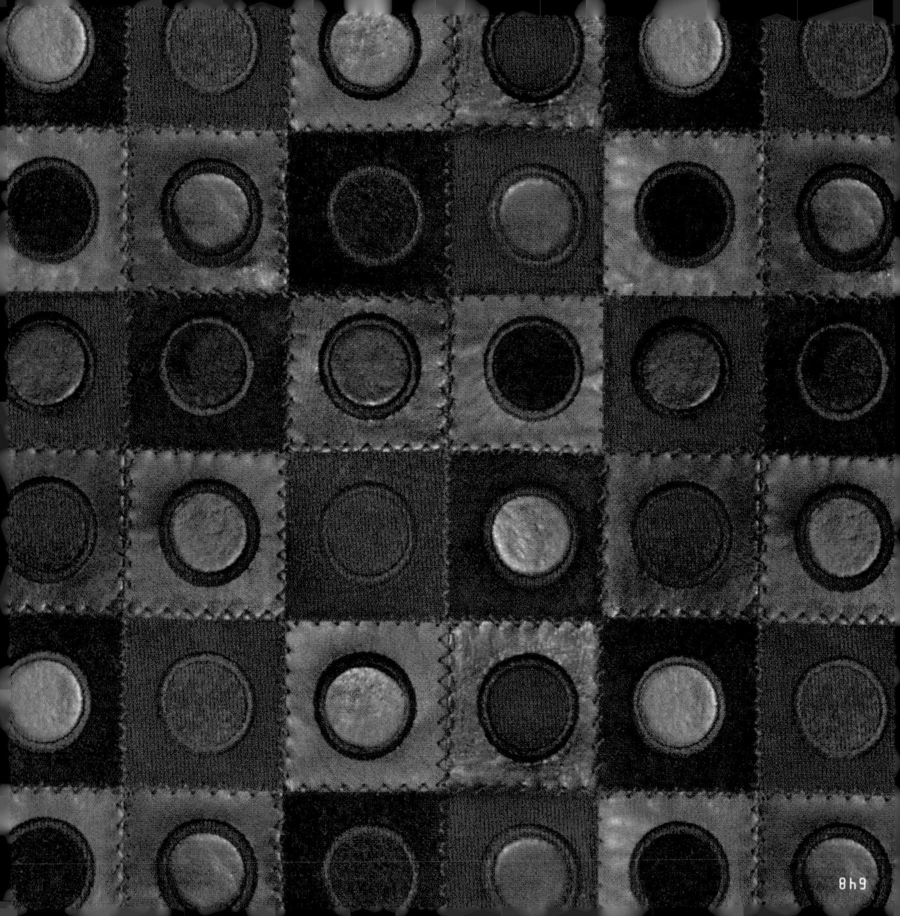

Myriam Lucas (GER) www.myaluc.de

Myriam Lucas (GER) www.myaluc.de

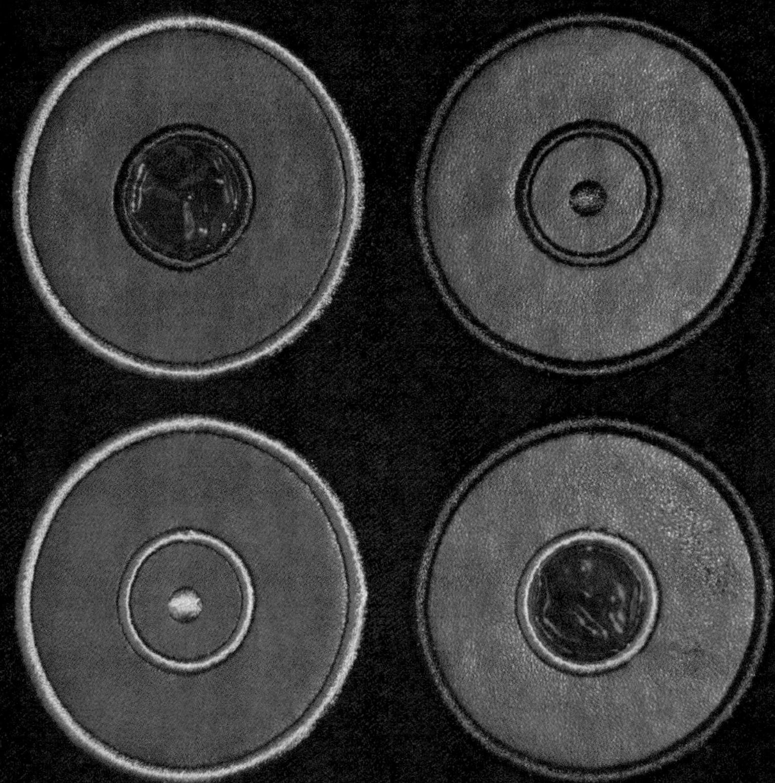

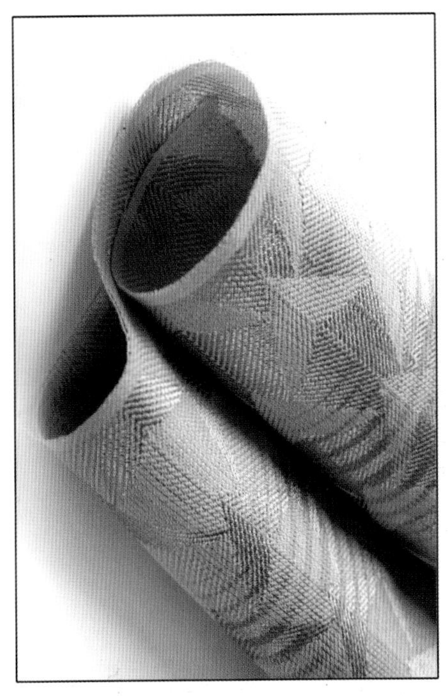

Suse Brand (GER) susebrand@gmx.net

index

all featured designers in alphabetical order

Surname , Prename	Loc.	Contact
10am	(GRE)	acaciafalcata@gmail.com www.myspace.com/10antemeridiem
Aalbers, Bart	(NED)	bart@bartaalbers.com www.bartaalbers.com
Aer	(TW)	www.flickr.com/photos/cotton120
Arcioli, Olivier	(ARG)	info@olivier-jean-sebastian.com www.o-j-s.com
Axmann, Stefanie	(GER)	info@stefanieaxmann.com www. stefanieaxmann.com
Becichi, Florina	(ROU)	florina_jasmine1@yahoo.com www.behance.net/florina
Bauer, Vanessa	(GER)	www.sloveroccoco.wordpress.com
Berrie, Christine	(GBR)	info@christineberrie.com www.christineberrie.com
Bertell, Erik	(FIN)	erik@kaamosgroup.fi www.kaamosgroup.fi
Blanchard, Marie	(FRA)	marie-blanchard@hotmail.fr www.marieblanchard.com
Brand, Suse	(GER)	susebrand@gmx.net
Brand, Suse & Hoffmann, Juliane	(GER)	susebrand@gmx.net
Boomkens, Denise	(NED)	info@deniseboomkens.nl
Boso, Allie	(USA)	allie07421@aol.com www.noregrets.bigcartel.com
Brehm, Lara	(FRA)	mail@larabrehm.com www.larabrehm.blogspot.com
Budny, Jens	(GER)	mail@jensbudny.de www.jensbudny.de
Büttel, Leslie	(SUI)	lesliebuettel@gmail.com
Byk, Mark	(USA)	www.monstermeans.com
Cambareri, Fiorella Carla	(ARG)	fiocamba_512@hotmail.com
Campelo, Wagner	(BRA)	wcampelo@gmail.com www.wagnercampelo.com
Churchill, Jessie	(GBR)	www.flickr.com/photos/jessiechurchill

Pages

Surname , Prename	Loc.	Contact
Crla, David	(CZE)	info@davidcrla.com www.davidcrla.com
Dabner, Thomas	(GBR)	tom.dabner@gmail.com www.fivesandzeros.blogspot.com
Devetak, Tanja	(SLO)	tanja.devetak@siol.net www.devetka.carbonmade.com
Dietrich, Anne	(GER)	contact@hatgirl.de
Eichler, Annette	(GER)	info@annette-eichler.de www.annette-eichler.de
Evans, Lloyd	(GBR)	lloyd@designhousestudios.co.uk www.designhousestudios.co.uk
Fayek, Catherine	(GER)	catherine.fayek@web.de
Fliess, Tomás	(ARG)	contacto@nnss.com.ar www.aupowerinside.com
Fontagnier, Pablo	(GER)	www.digitalplayground.de
Fort, Denise	(NZL)	info@fort-denise.com www.fort-illustrations.com
Fouad, Mohamed	(EG)	www.fvad.deviantart.com
Franco, Julia & Renata	(MEX)	juliayrenata@yahoo.com www.iqons.com/juliayrenata
Frederiksen, T. & Fuglsang, J.	(DEN)	youhadme@shoethebear.com www.shoethebear.com
Friedrich, Mike	(GER)	info@mike-friedrich.com www.mike-friedrich.com
Fuchs, Rebecca	(NED)	rf-becks@gmx.de www.casadelzorro.de
Galtsova, Irina	(RUS)	irina.galtsova@gmail.ru
Girod, Nadja	(GER)	nadja.girod@gmail.com www.nadjagirod.com
Glitschka, Von	(USA)	von@glitschka.com www.vonglitschka.com
Gmeiner, Ulla	(GER)	ugmeiner@yahoo.de www.telaire.blogspot.com
Goh, Sabrina	(SIN)	www.sabrinagoh.com
Graf, Patricia Yasmine	(GER)	info@pyg-design.de www.pyg-design.de
Greco, Monica	(ITA)	www.envelop.eu/shop/monica-greco

Pages

Surname , Prename	Loc.	Contact
Halleck, Silvio	(BRA)	www.halleck.com.br
Hamala, Anukun	(THA)	info@nokhookdesign.com www.nokhookdesign.com
Hartikainen, Isa	(GER)	isa.hartikainen@gmail.com
Hofacker, Sandra	(SUI)	info@apfel-z.de www.apfel-z.de
Holm, Martin	(NOR)	mail@martinholm.com www.martinholm.com
Horrocks, Rachel	(GBR)	rachel@rachelhorrocks.com www.rachelhorrocks.com
Horsman, Natalie	(GBR)	www.le-petit-oiseau.blogspot.com
Hoyer, Laura	(USA)	laura@openfacesandwich.com www.openfacesandwich.com
Jacobi, Marie	(GER)	info@marie-jacobi.de www.marie-jacobi.de
Jaspers, Silke	(GER)	info@cafe-lala.de www.cfae-lala.de
Jeanne, Audrey	(FRA)	ilovedrawing@orange.fr www.audreyjeanne.blogspot.com
Johansson, Emma	(AUS)	emma@emmasink.com www.emmasink.com
Jordan, Martin	(GBR)	martin@manss.com www.manss.com
Kaljuvee, Kätlin	(EE)	katlinkaljuvee@gmail.com
Kama	(INA)	www.oxidizzy.com
Kaneda	(ITA)	kaneda@nosurprises.it www.nosurprises.it
Karaca, Zeynep	(GBR)	info@figgi.net www.figgi.net
Kettner, Florian	(GER)	info@rv20.com www.rv20.com
Kimberling, Josephine	(USA)	www.josephinekimberling.com
Kloszynski, Jenny	(NED)	goplant@gmx.de www.goplant.eu
Knaack, Alex	(GER)	alex@born-clothing.de www.bxp.bigcartel.com
Kunkel, Ulrike	(GER)	u.kunkel@gmx.net www.ritapita.de

Pages

Surname , Prename	Loc.	Contact
Kuo, River	(TPE)	a8river@yahoo.com.tw www.riverkuo.com
Kuokka, Jenni	(FI)	jenni@hahmo.fi
Kurochkina, Katja	(GER)	tkanikurik@yahoo.com www.kurochkina.com
Layko (Lay Sedlakova)	(SVK)	Lay.Sedlakova@gmail.com
Lear, Jason	(GBR)	jason@quickonthedraw.co.uk www.jasonlearillustration.co.uk
Ledwith, Mariano	(ARG)	m_ledwith@hotmail.com www. www.flickr.com/photos/soygros
Leibenguth, Finna	(GER)	finna@wg-atelier.de www.wg-atelier.de
Lemke, Harri	(GER)	www.designbuero-lemke.de
Lucas, Myriam	(GER)	info@myaluc.de www.myaluc.de
Mackenzie, Joel	(CAN)	joelamackenzie@gmail.com www.ijoelamackenzie@gmail.com
Malikova, Lubov	(UKR)	lubov.malikova@gmail.com www.flickr.com/photos/luba_ma
Marchionna, Sandra	(GER)	sandra.marchionna@freenet.de
Markovic, Kristina	(GER)	info@kristinamarkovic.com www.kristinamarkovic.com
Marquez, Rene	(CAN)	renemarquez@yahoo.com www.rene-marquez.com
Mauruschat, Nikolas	(GER)	info@omprod.eu www.omprod.eu
Meiying, Lydia	(BGR)	lydia@hellomeiying.com www.hellomeiying.com
Meyle, Tanja	(GER)	nfo@meylenstein.net www.meylenstein.net
Mihr, Florian	(GER)	info@johnnylove.de www.sk80s.com
Mitte, Eike	(GER)	info@vectorian.de www.vectorian.de
Müller, Christian Frank	(GER)	cfmrex@web.de
Müller, Sabrina	(GER)	hello@sabrinamueller.com www.sabrinamueller.com
Nouanesing, John	(FRA)	contact@johnnouanesing.fr www.johnnouanesing.fr

Pages

Surname , Prename	Loc.	Contact
Nerk Collective	(ITA)	info@nerk.it www.nerk.it
Officina Disturbo	(ITA)	www.officinadisturbo.org
Paccagnella, Fabrizio	(ITA)	info@spritzer.it www.spritzer.it
Petrova, Nadya	(RUS)	nadyape@gmail.com www.flickr.com/people/sheepdeer
Pfriem, Eva	(GER)	Evapfriem@web.de
Pierdicca, Lorella	(ITA)	ll@lldesign.it www.lldesign.it
Poortman, Remona	(NED)	remonapoortman@gmail.com www.remona-poortman.blogspot.
Prien, Marc	(GER)	info@empegra.de www.empegra.de
Ramirez, Pablo	(ARG)	www.pabloramirez.com
Rewel, Janinel	(FIN)	janine@janinerewell.com www.janinerewell.com
Ricci, Ivan	(ITA)	kawaiimind@gmail.com www.kawaii-style.net
RiotCreations	(GER)	service@riotcreations.com www.riotcreations.com
Rölle, Julio	(GER)	hello@44flavours.de www.44flavours.de
Rüter, Anne	(GER)	www.neoterisch.com
Sanchez, Suz	(ESP)	hello@suzsanchez.com www.suzsanchez.com
Schroeder, Kai	(GER)	ks-schroeder@gmx.de
Schuster, Dennis	(GER)	dxtr@gmx.net www.flickr.com/photos/dxtrs
Sferlazzo, Rossella	(ITA)	rossella.sferlazzo@email.it www.sferlazzorossella.wordpress.co
Sichelstiel, Eva	(GER)	eva@sichi.de eva@sichi.de
Stehle, Simon	(GER)	info@bloodgold.de www.bloodgold.de
Stohrer, Véronique	(GER)	info@veronique-stohrer.com www.veronique-stohrer.com

Pages

Surname , Prename	Loc	Contact
Stølan, Sylvia	(NED)	mail@sylviastolan.com www.sylviastolan.com
Studiocharlie	(ITA)	www.studiocharlie.org
Szamosi, Attila	(GER)	info@peachbeach.de www.peachbeach.de
Täschner, Caroline	(GER)	caroline.taeschner@gmx.de
Tasoz, Aylin	(NED)	atasoz@gmail.com
Tekneya , Vartan & Paleit, Lilo	(GER)	vartan@ted-and-rose.com www.ted-and-rose.com
Tischendorf, Uta	(GER)	utatischendorf@gmx.de
Torrontegui Palacios, Itxaso	(GER)	itxaso.torrontegui@gmail.com www.itxasotorrontegui.blogspot
Tortora, Mark Byk & Kristine	(CAN)	info@ampersandampersand.com www.ampersandampersand.c
Tratz, Matthias	(GER)	matthias@hkant.de www.hkant.de
Tuominen, Jenni	(FIN)	jenni@sorsapukki.fi www.sorsapukki.fi
UREDD	(NOR)	www.uredd.no
Varga, Arina	(ROU)	www.arinavarga.ro
Vault49	(USA)	www.vault49.com
Villodres, Alicia	(ESP)	www. alicia-villodres.blogspot.com
Vogel, Sabrina	(AUT)	katjara@ymail.com www.sabrinavogel.com
von Moos, linus	(SUI)	linus@ripsl.ch www.ripsl.ch
Wade, Sarah	(GBR)	sarah@designhousestudios.co.uk www.designhousestudios.co.
Weier, Andre	(GER)	info@nalindesign.com www.nalindesign.com
Wunderlich, Lars	(GER)	info@peachbeach.de www.peachbeach.de
Ximena, Escobar	(COL)	escobar.ximena@gmail.com www.ximenaescobar.com
Yakushova, Yulia	(RUS)	bang@bangbangstudio.ru www.bangbangstudio.ru
Zayoba	(GER)	zayoba@the-artillery.de www.zayoba.de

Pages